HOW TO MAKE YOUR FAMILY BUSINESS LAST

Techniques, Advice, Checklists, and Resources for Keeping the Family Business in the Family

By
MITZI PERDUE

ISBN 978-1-884-108-07-5

Published October 2017
R. J. Myers Publishing Company,
Washington, D.C.

Book Design by Initial Design & Media
Photography by Helene Delillo
Book Cover by Jessie Batilo

HOW TO MAKE YOUR FAMILY BUSINESS LAST

This book is dedicated to the academics who study family businesses and the advisors who help members of family businesses get past the predictable and unpredictable problems they'll encounter. You do so much good in such an important realm that my wish is, "May your tribe increase!"

Mitzi Perdue, Salisbury, MD

INTRODUCTION

The Best Investment A Business Family Can Make

Whatever the size of your family business, and whatever your race, creed, religion, or nationality, one of the best investments you can make is cultivating a loving, high-functioning family. After all, our deepest pains and our deepest joys are likely to come from our families. In a family business, that's true whether we're in our 20s or 90s.

In theory, you can't put a price on family harmony. However, I've seen that it can be worth more than every penny a person owns. I intend to show that taking the time and effort needed to cultivate a high-functioning family is the best investment any of us can make. And I know of at least one point where family harmony would have been worth a billion dollars.

The Two Billion Dollar Argument

To see what I mean, come back with me to the day before Thanksgiving, a year ago. Karla Adams and I were walking up Madison Avenue. (I'm not using her real name, but the amount of money I'll be talking about is real.)

With the holidays right around the corner, the storefront windows were decorated with evergreens, dancing elves, cotton snow, and twinkling lights. Karla and I darted between the shoppers, some of whom were so laden with parcels and bags that they could hardly see where they were going.

I leaned over towards Karla and said, "It's such a happy time of year! I can't wait to share it with my family at Thanksgiving!"

I was beaming, imagining the 50 or so of the family members gathered around the five long tables that it takes to hold us all, and then in my imagination I glimpsed the sideboard laden with turkey, chicken, mashed potatoes, green beans, sweet potato biscuits …. But then as I looked over at Karla, I saw her expression was changing.

She was now pale, and her walk had become stiff, as if she were in pain.

"Karla, what's wrong?" I quickly asked.

"Mitzi," she sighed, 'I wish *I* had a family to go home to."

"But you have a brother? Can't you spend Thanksgiving with him?"

"No!" she answered with a vehemence that surprised me. She fingered the fringe of the blue scarf around her neck and added, "I never told you, but Joe and I haven't spoken since 2014. The last time we saw each other was in court, arguing about our inheritance."

I gasped. "Oh no! That's awful!" I couldn't imagine a family bond so irreparably broken as to force me to spend Thanksgiving alone. "Isn't there something you could do to put things back together again?"

"He testified about me in court," said Karla. She spoke slowly, and the bitterness in her voice weighed down every word. "He lied. To get a bigger share of our inheritance, *he lied.* He cared more about the money than he cared about me."

She paused for a moment, as if remembering the court case, maybe even reliving it. She spoke through pursed lips, "When Joseph lied about me, he torched all our bridges."

I stared at her, horrified. This terrible thing had happened to my friend, and I'd never known until now.

Karla continued. "Our parents left us each a billion dollars, but you know what? I'd give every penny of it if only… *if only* I were like you and had a family to go home to."

I told you a moment ago that in theory it would be hard to put a price on family harmony. But here's one person who told me she would give *a billion dollars* to have a family.

Think about this for a moment. *Your deepest happiness or your deepest misery will come from your intimate relationships.* When these relationships go badly, the pain can permeate every hour of every day.

Money can't make up for that. What good does it do to succeed financially if you fail as a family?

HOW TO MAKE YOUR FAMILY BUSINESS LAST

Succeeding Financially and Failing
As A Family

When the family quarrel involves a family business, the consequences are even worse. When there's a family quarrel, businesses can go "China Syndrome." That's the term family business expert Thomas William Deans uses in his book *Every Family's Business*.

The phrase "China Syndrome" comes from the 1979 disaster movie of the same name. The film starred Jane Fonda and Michael Douglas as witnesses to a nuclear power plant's emergency shutdown.

To explain what the term has come to mean in business, Deans writes, "When a family business goes China Syndrome, it doesn't explode, it implodes and quietly melts into a big, deep, dark hole in the ground where the business used to be."

He goes on to say that family businesses can be leveled in weeks if not days. And it happens every day.

In the view of Deans most family businesses are ticking time bombs. And he's right. Only about 3% of family businesses make it past the third generation. Family quarrels are the major reason families fail.

That's the bad news.

The good news is it doesn't have to be that way.

HOW TO MAKE YOUR FAMILY BUSINESS LAST

Few Things Are More Important Than A High Functioning Family

Investing the thought, time, and energy to create close and enduring family relationships is one of the most important things a family can do. I'll be sharing with you here tools that can help you build a culture that keeps your family together across the generations.

The information comes from firsthand observations of two families which have been together for a combined total of 224 years. My family of origin, the Henderson family, started as the Henderson Estate Company in 1890. This company grew into the Sheraton Hotel chain, and our family is still intact 127 years later.

The family I married into, Perdue Farms, began as a breakfast egg company in 1920, and we're just three years short of celebrating our 100th anniversary.

The biggest secret for their longevity is this: Neither the Hendersons nor the Perdues left their family's continuation to chance. Both families put time and energy into creating a culture that supports keeping the family together.

What Does A High Functioning Family Look Like?

Every family has a culture, but a high-functioning family has a culture with the following characteristics:

- Family members enjoy being together.

- They support each other.

- They want to help one another to be their best selves.

- They are aware of the enormous benefits of belonging to a close family.

Members of a high-functioning family understand that:

- For a family to work, members can't expect always to get their way. Compromise is key.

- Each family member must support the family and at times make sacrifices for the family.

- Membership in the family is not a one-way street. You don't get the benefit of your family's financial and social benefits without owing a lot in return.

- The elders are responsible for teaching the younger family members the attitudes and values that will give them the greatest chance at happiness and fulfillment.

Members of a family that leave their culture to chance are in danger of the following:

- Parents focus on the business and making a living, but don't invest in the family's culture.

- Parents don't teach the younger members of the family that they are there to support one another.

- Family members fail to appreciate the warmth and love a family can provide.

- Family members don't learn that sometimes you have a choice between having a relationship and being right, and if you choose being right over having a relationship, you are sacrificing a lot of what makes life joyous.

- Family members do not learn until it is too late that losing your family over something like an inheritance issue is probably the worst choice you could possibly make.

For families to be a success over time, individual family members will need to give up something of themselves for the benefit of the larger family group. A person may be entirely right about an issue, but when Thanksgiving comes along and he or she is all alone, is hanging onto "being right" worth it?

Since family harmony can be worth every penny you have, how do you go about establishing a family culture that supports family harmony? How do you respond to the predictable–and unpredictable–crises that are likely to come your way?

That, dear friends, is what the rest of this book is about. Every family has a culture. The cultures that come about by design have a far better chance of surviving than the ones that came about by default. What follows are suggestions for ways of creating and strengthening a culture that supports keeping your family together across the generations.

SECTION I

STRENGTHEN THE CULTURE: IT WASN'T RAINING WHEN NOAH BUILT THE ARK.

INTRODUCTION

Your family's culture is the biggest tool you have available for keeping the family business in the family. It's at the basis of everything you do because at heart, a family's culture is "the way we do things." I put the section on strengthening the culture first because it's the foundation for everything else.

However, if you are in a difficult situation right now (and frankly, the odds are that you may be, given that conflicts can arise so easily in any family), then skip ahead to the next section of this book, the one on PROBLEMS? DON'T LET THEM TURN INTO THREE-GENERATION TRAGEDIES. (Page 96) That section offers first aid for a number of problems you may be up against, including in particular, conflicts that threaten relationships or even the entire company.

The section you're reading now is about creating, building, maintaining, and handing on a positive family culture. Members of your family may be only barely conscious of the family's culture, but it underlies what family members feel is right and wrong and what is worth doing or not worth doing.

You want a vibrant family culture because a family-supporting culture can prevent many of the issues that can tear families apart. A strong family culture can help over-ride the centrifugal forces that come from society at large, the forces that tend to pull families away from each other and that make individuals forget they're part of something bigger than themselves.

A positive culture doesn't just happen; it's important to know and use the tools that make it happen. And I, as someone who cares that your family does well, hope you find these tools useful. They've helped my families and they can help yours.

CHAPTER 1

The Individual Versus the Family: A Tug of War, But, Family Has To Come First

There never has been and never will be a family that can avoid all conflicts. That's because there's a built-in tug-of-war in families: it's the tug-of-war between being an individual and belonging to the family group.

On the individualism side, we are pulled towards wanting to be able to express ourselves as we see fit and to act on our own true, authentic feelings. We want to feel autonomous and free; we don't want to feel repressed or smothered.

On the family side, we yearn for a ready-made source of comfort, support, understanding, security, and identity. Ah, but that can require giving up some of our individualism in return for conforming to the norms of the group.

Members of any family are likely to feel pulled between these two forces. However, being part of a business family changes the balance because in this case, there's a greater responsibility to the group.

It's Different When You're In a Family Business

When you're a member of a family business, there's a lot more at stake than just the family. There's an entire world of others who are influenced by how the family is doing, including employees, stockholders, lenders, customers, and countless others who may be affected by the health of the family business.

HOW TO MAKE YOUR FAMILY BUSINESS LAST

The thing is, a happy family means a happy company. And alas, a miserable family can mean a wounded company. This means, family members need to learn from early on to listen to other points of view and that compromise is key

Standing on principal sounds like a good idea, but it can end up devastating the family. A person who won't compromise is highly likely to enable his or her lawyer to buy a new car while at the same time blowing up the family.

And that's not the end. A public quarrel can harm or even kill a business. When I was growing up as a member of the family that founded the Sheraton Hotels, I was told from infancy that a public quarrel could harm the family business. That led to a deeply culturally ingrained notion that public quarrels "are not something we do."

My siblings and I grew up with the phrase, repeated a thousand times, "We don't wash our dirty linen in public." We'd hear this during meals, or during holiday rituals, or when we'd hear stories about our grandparents and others who had gone before.

We were made aware that with 20,000 employees and 25,000 stockholders, it would be WRONG to let quarrels escalate. We knew that a public family quarrel could mean we'd be vulnerable to competitors; it would be demoralizing to the employees; it would harm the brand. We were also told that since Sheraton stock was publicly traded, a public family quarrel could cause Sheraton stock to plummet. That would mean widows and orphans would be suffering because of our selfishness.

HOW TO MAKE YOUR FAMILY BUSINESS LAST

The mantra of, "We do not wash our dirty linen in public" was so firmly ingrained that I don't think any of us ever considered bringing in a lawyer or a member of the press. We knew to keep quarrels from escalating.

The Principle Gets Put to a Test

And by the way, we did have issues. To take just one, in 1968, some of the family members wanted to take advantage of a tremendous offer that ITT had made to buy the Sheraton chain. It would mean enormous amounts of cash right now.

However, several of us including me didn't want this to happen. Those who opposed it all had our reasons.

"It's my identity!"

"It's disrespectful to Father's memory!"

"I don't want the cash; I want to be a part of Sheraton!"

"An outside company will never care as much about the welfare of the employees as we do!"

Imagine for a moment the feelings involved: your family is divided over the possibility of large amounts of immediate cash; a large part of your identity is in danger of being ripped away; your parents' legacy is being turned over to outsiders! It's a great big bubbling stew of some of your strongest feelings. In the case of me and my siblings, emotions were at white-hot levels.

We Kept It Secret

We argued among ourselves, but none of us ever spoke

to lawyers or the press. I don't think anyone outside the family knew what we were feeling.

In the end, we did sell Sheraton. To the rest of the world, we had a united front, and we were true to our deeply held values, that we never washed our dirty linen in public.

I think at the end of this experience, we all felt proud that we had gotten through this and remained a close family. Once the decision was made, we closed ranks and nobody held a grudge.

We're still a united family half a century later. But this wouldn't have happened if we hadn't developed a culture ahead of time that supported "family first" and "We don't wash our dirty linen in public."

Since conflicts are inevitable, the best strategy is to prepare for them ahead of time.

The most helpful preparation is, develop a solid culture of "putting the family first." This doesn't come about automatically.

Checklist for Putting Family First

Take a moral stand that it's wrong to move quarrels outside the family. There are so many others who could get hurt by a public quarrel that it's morally wrong to allow a family business quarrel to become public. In the Henderson family, we learned public quarrels were wrong in the same way we learned murder was wrong.

Have a phrase that children hear continuously that reinforces "Family First" Continuously emphasize that we don't take quarrels outside the family. The Henderson mantra sure worked for us: "We don't wash our dirty linen in public."

Put relationships ahead of ego. Let family members know from a young age that there are times when you have a choice of getting your way or having a relationship, and that it's a terrible bargain to sacrifice one of the most important parts of your life for the ego gratification of getting your way.

When there's conflict, make sure that everyone gets heard and listened to. Being heard goes a long way toward defusing conflict.

Teach family members to avoid being addicted to being right. Being addicted to being right is ego-centric and destructive. A milder way of saying the same thing is, "Don't be stubborn." Don't reward family members for being stubborn,

Be careful what you say in anger. Angry words can be self-fulfilling, such as for example, threats of divorce or disinheritance. You say them in momentary anger, but the person hearing them may remember them for a lifetime. As my brother Barclay Henderson warns, "Garbage can come out of Pandora's Box that can't be stuffed back in again."

CHAPTER 2

Traditions: The Lifeblood of Identity

I once asked the 70 members of the Henderson Clan to write an essay on "What it means to be us." My purpose was to use their answers as the basis for a book celebrating our 127th year of getting together as a family.

Virtually every one of their answers, which ranged in length from 100 words to 2000 words, mentioned the importance of family traditions. Most said that our tradition of getting together each year at the old family house in New Hampshire is one of the most meaningful parts of their lives, something they look forward to all year long.

Their answers to the "What it means to be us," question demonstrated to me the tight connection between identity and tradition. I saw that it's through traditions that we connect with our families and engage with our heritage. Tradition, I concluded, is the lifeblood of identity.

Of course, traditions aren't just reunions. Traditions are our rituals, ceremonies and the activities that we reliably do as a family through the years and across the generations.

They're an anchor in the changing sea of our life experiences. We get older, we go to school, we get jobs, people drift in and out of our lives, but our family traditions can continue through all our life stages as they continuously reinforce "What it means to be us."

HOW TO MAKE YOUR FAMILY BUSINESS LAST

Something that's particularly important to family businesses, traditions provide continuity between the generations. In view of which, cherish and strengthen your family traditions! Start new ones! And when families blend, adopt and support the traditions that the new family brings.

Some Traditions I Admire

• **Write birthday letters.** For almost five decades until his passing, Frank used to celebrate family birthdays by writing a long and meaningful handwritten letter to each child or grandchild on his or her birthday. Because he was a believer in being an inclusive family, he even wrote birthday letters to his step-children. I bet the youngsters receiving these were surprised by how much Frank knew about what was going on in their lives. Here he was, a busy captain of industry, yet he still communicated to each child, grandchild, and step-child how important they were to him. What must that do for a young person's self-confidence and self-worth? It's an easy thing to do. Try it!

• **At holiday events, review the family's history.** A family that I'm close to has a Christmas eve tradition that could be copied by any family business. This family has been extraordinarily successful in the movie business. On Christmas Eve, the family gathers around a dining room table that holds 30 people. The patriarch of the family provides bottles of a seriously expensive wine. The expensive wine signals that this dinner is an important event and sets the stage for people to give the event the attention it deserves. During dinner, the oldest members of the family go around the table reminding everyone how their family business got started. Ten or so family members recount details from the story that's been retold for generations, about how their immigrant ancestor started out as a farmer in New Jersey and then one day, the patriarch told his wife and children, "I'm tired of farming. We're moving to Hollywood." I think this family is fourth generation now, and the movies they've produced have been billion-dollar successes. Even so, they discuss values of frugality and hard work, and that the family wants to make sure that no member of this family is going to suffer from "rich man's disease," that is no one will be allowed to grow into an entitled snob. This Christmas Eve tradition is a fabulous time for embedding family history and family values.

• **Have wacky, unique ways of handling problems that the family can laugh about.** When I was a child and had some minor hurt, Mother would ask with mock seriousness, "Is it a square pain or a round pain?" As I focused on whether the pain in my stubbed toe was square or round, I regularly forgot the hurt. It was brilliant and she did it with my siblings as well. I did this with my children and today I do it with my grandchildren. In my family, we're people who have pains that are either square or round, and the sheer wackiness of this is a tradition we all cherish and laugh over.

• **Have favorite meals.** My father, co-founder of the Sheraton Hotel Chain, and someone whom some of the finest chefs in the world wanted to impress, created a tradition of Sunday night dinner that had to have been unique. He'd always make the same thing for mother and me and my siblings: Nabisco Shredded Wheat with hot evaporated milk poured over it. It was a remarkably simple meal, and light years away from the fare he would normally consume. I think what we loved most was the sheer incongruity of someone who regularly consumed some of the finest meals chefs could create, enjoying something so simple. We adored this tradition.

• **Have a yearly talent show.** In the Henderson Family at our yearly reunion, we have "Saturday Night Live at Knollwood." All year family members prepare songs or ballet or practice their instruments or make videos, or write poetry prepare for the event. It's something we think about all year long and then we talk about the evening after its over for another year. This tradition gets everyone thinking about the family and how proud we are of each other's talents.

• **Have a Family Home Evening.** As described by Brett McKay in the Art of Manliness, Mormons are encouraged to set aside one night per week for Family Home Evening (FHE). A typical FHE includes a fun activity and a short lesson or devotional on some virtue or scripture. A FHE is usually capped off with a special treat. The goal of the FHE is to teach your children the principles and values you want them to carry with them as adults, all within an informal and loving atmosphere. It's a tradition that can be adapted by families of any religious stripe or families who aren't religious. There's no formula for Family Home Evening. As McKay recommends, just corral the kids for 30 minutes one night a week for fun, discussion, and eats.

Checklist for Possible Family Traditions

Ideally you come up with your own, or even better, continue ones you already have. The list that follows can be a jumping off point for thinking about your own possible traditions.

Evening Walks

Eating dinner together

HOW TO MAKE YOUR FAMILY BUSINESS LAST

Holding hands while saying a blessing

Prayers at night

Reading stories at bedtime

At dinner, tell what happened each day

Special breakfast Sunday morning

Lunch or dinner at a restaurant after religious services

Family Games.

I grew up with card games or "What did they put in the old man's soup."

On birthday's, the child gets to pick the menu

Moon watching parties

Perseid shower watching nights

In my family, we'd spend the night in sleeping bags on the lawn when the Perseid meteor showers would be occurring towards the end of summer. Appreciating nature's wonders together was fabulously bonding for all ages.

Scrapbook for each child

This is a long-term project, but from the time they are babies, collect photos in a scrapbook that you'll give to them on their 21st birthday. Over the years, include photos and captions with their friends' names and where the photos were taken.

Write these names because 15 years later, you may not remember the names of the others who're in the pictures. My kids say the Age 21 Scrapbook was the best present they ever got.

Have older family members write their autobiographies.

This is probably not right for many families, but with the Hendersons, we're expected to write an autobiography if we're older than 60. Since this has been going on for generations, I bet we've got 50 of biographies, and it provides an extraordinary view of who we are and where we came from. Some are short, such as 20 pages and some are in four large volumes.

Resources:

See page 76 of this book for chapter on *Family Glue: What It Means to Be Us* for directions on how to create your own *What It Means to Be Us* book.

The Art of Manliness is so rich in content and clever and useful that I wish I could make a visit there mandatory. Go to: http://www.artofmanliness.com.
The Art of Manliness section on Family Home Evenings is here: http://www.artofmanliness.com/2013/10/16/60-family-tradition-ideas/

Pinterest.com is great for inspiration. Search on "family traditions" or "holiday traditions," or any kind of tradition that interests you.

CHAPTER 3

Plan Time Together: You Can't Love What You Don't Know

One of the biggest reason the Henderson and Perdue families have continued for a combined total of 224 years is: both families invest time in being with each other. If you want the family culture to continue, then it's crucial for family members to get together and experience the values they live by.

E.O. Wilson, the great Harvard biologist, says that it is impossible to love, cherish and protect something if you don't know about it. He was referring to endangered species, but the thought applies equally to families.

We have to get to know each other if we're going to love, cherish and protect our family. That means spending time together. For deposits in the *Bank of Family Closeness*, there are few things that top being physically together.

An endowed family vacation may be the best way to accomplish this goal. Recognizing this, back in 1890, the Henderson patriarch John Henderson endowed a yearly get-together. Frank Perdue likewise left funds so that his descendants could count on scheduled times to be together.

Something that I remember from Frank's and my wedding day: a friend noticed that at the reception afterwards, 12 of Frank's grandchildren were playing on the lawn in front of my house. The friend said, "They all know each other! They're all playing together! It's as if they speak their own shorthand language!"

The reason I remember this from almost three decades ago is that I was surprised that my friend was surprised. I expect cousins to know each other. But then I realized that not everyone has regular reunions, and cousins don't necessarily know each other well.

If you're a multi-generational family and aren't already having regularly scheduled time to spend at least several days a year in each other's company, then please consider it.

And if you are already doing it, and if you're the patriarch or matriarch, how about endowing these events so they'll continue in the future? I'm not sure what could be a better investment for deposits in the *Bank of Family Closeness* than endowing family vacations as far into the future as possible.

Today there's an extraordinary range of possibilities for you and your family members. How about considering some of these?

Types of Vacations

- **Ancestry Trip.** One of the best Henderson Family trips I was ever on was when we went to visit the homes of family members in England and Wales. At the end of the trip, everyone knew riveting stories about where we came from. It was bonding in a never-to-be-forgotten way.

- **Digital Detox.** I haven't tried this, but I have friends who have done it and who swear by it. The goal is to go somewhere for a few days where there are no screens. That means no laptops, no TV, no cell phones, no iPads. For both my families this would be a hard sell, but your family might be among those who would love it.

- **Volunteering Trip**. I know families that regularly do this and it's apparently incredibly bonding. You work all day long on, for instance, repairing a home in Appalachia, and at the end, I'm told, you have a fabulous sense of having worked together for a common goal. There's also the self-esteem that comes from knowing you've helped someone else or done something important for the environment. Do a Google search on "volunteer vacations," and you'll find an assortment of local or overseas possibilities.

- **See the USA**. Some of the Perdues' best vacations have been to national parks. It's a wonderful way not only of strengthening your own family legacy, it's also a way of appreciating the far-sightedness of citizens who long ago saw the value of creating our National Parks system.

- **Cruises.** I'm particularly a fan of river cruises because there's so much to see each day and there's no danger of seasickness. If the family is made up of history buffs, there's a fabulous Mississippi cruise where the paddle wheel boat schedules its stops to coincide with Civil War recreations. For more choices, try http://themecruisefinder.com and you'll see more than 500 themed cruises, whether it's Star Wars at Sea or fitness or art lovers or astronomy. Or simply Google "cruises for families" and you'll see hundreds and hundreds of possibilities.

HOW TO MAKE YOUR FAMILY BUSINESS LAST

Checklist for Planning a Family Vacation

Eighteen Months to Two Years ahead of Time

> **Decide who is in charge**.
> In the Perdue Family this rotates, and typically, it's the married-ins who volunteer. Most often there are two co-chairs. In the Henderson family, it's usually the same people for decades at a time.
>
> **Check out TripAdvisor.com**
> Also do a Google search on "best websites for group travel." You'll find reviews of the various apps and websites that can help you find destinations that accommodate groups. Available apps and sites can also help make reservations and later, they can track the responses from members of your group about their travel arrangements, what activities they want to sign up for, and dietary preferences.
>
> **Decide the location.**
> The family can vote on the location or alternatively, the organizers can be given the task of making the decision. (In the Perdue family we've done both, and both methods seem to work equally well. However, having the organizers make the decision is simpler and faster.)
>
> **Hire a travel agent, maybe.**
> Whether you do or not depends on how much experience family members have with this and how much time they're willing to put into it. With both the Hendersons and the Perdues, our family vacations are generally a do-it-yourself affair. However, in favor of travel agents, they may be able to suggest amazing places you

wouldn't have thought of, and they can spare you a lot of paperwork and hassle.

Decide the location.
The family can vote on the location or alternatively, the organizers can be given the task of making the decision. (In the Perdue family we've done both, and both methods seem to work equally well. However, having the organizers make the decision is simpler and faster.)

Book the Venue.
Popular places that can accommodate a large family may be filled up years in advance. You'll find that even a year ahead of time, many of the places you might like to go will already be filled, or at least past the point where they can accommodate a couple of dozen people on the dates that you want. Some of the world class ones like Necker Island are likely to be booked during the Christmas holidays as much as decades ahead of time.

Twelve Months ahead of Time

Start booking the activities at the venue.
If there are only a few of you and it's not a popular activity or a popular resort, this can wait.

Six Months ahead of Time

Start making travel arrangements for family members.

Create an activities spread sheet and e-mail it to everyone, with "Here's the activities list and tell me what you want to do."
Alternatively use one of the group travel apps or

websites, and invite family members to edit it, adding their on-line information, for arrival times, and preferred activities.

Maybe, hire a professional family advisor to give a talk one evening.
The talk may be on some question of interest to the family, such as governance or decision-making or investing. The family vacation can be a great time for family education as well as family fun.

Check all necessary documents.
If there will be overseas travel, double check that everyone's passports and visas are up-to-date. As my good friend Robin Tauck from the travel company Tauck, Inc, says, "Remember, you cannot travel on travel dates with a passport that expires within 90 days of your expected travel time. Don't be left at the gate!" She's seen this happen to even the most experienced travelers, so pay special attention to having at least 90 days left before expiration on all family passports before you leave.

Three Months ahead of Time

Plan a family an evening at the beginning or end of the trip. I recommend using this time for presenting a 'Service to the Family Award' to whomever has been in charge of the family trip. He or she or they will have put in more time than people would guess, and recognizing them can be a nice family tradition.

Book babysitters at the venue

HOW TO MAKE YOUR FAMILY BUSINESS LAST

One Month ahead of time

Check up on travel plans.

Reconfirm baby sitting

Plan Menus Check dietary concerns for any family member.

Reconfirm who is doing which activity at what time.

Alert people what they'll need to pack, including any equipment that might be needed

One Week ahead of Time

Send e-mail with weather information

Resources:
- www.Tripadvisor.com
- http://themecruisefinder.com
- http://www.familyvacationcritic.com/13-free-travel-apps-for-families/art/ I haven't used a travel app so I can't recommend one but if you'll search on "Family Travel Apps" you'll find dozens of pages of possibilities. This source I just mentioned caught my eye, and it could serve as a starting point for you.

.

CHAPTER 4

Philanthropy, Antidote to the Notion "The World Revolves Around Me"

Take a moment to think of something important that you can do to help your family business endure across the generations. For the purpose of this question, choose a factor that includes all family members, not just those who work in the family business.

Have you thought about it?

OK, here's one answer, and it may be the best: encourage family members to engage in philanthropic activities together.

One of The Most Reliable and Effective Tools for Promoting Family Glue

Creating a legacy of family philanthropy is one of the most reliable, most effective, and most engaging tools for keeping members of a family business together. I've seen it work in both the Henderson and Perdue families.

Both families engage in charitable giving and I've seen that while being charitable is about benefitting others, the benefits to the families are incalculable. Philanthropy helps confer one of the strongest factors in keeping a family together, and that factor is, identity. Identity provides shared purpose and a sense of "This is who we are, this is what it means to be us."

Frank understood this. I once asked him how he felt

about charitable giving. His answer was one I make it my business to have the younger members of the family hear frequently: "My wish for future generations is that they be known as good citizens and contributing members of the community in which they live." He knew that this would be bonding.

Philanthropic Giving Encourages Thinking Unselfishly

This attitude means members of the family realize that they're part of something bigger than themselves. It gets them thinking unselfishly. It gets them thinking what they can do for others, not just what the family can do for them. And that, by the way, is one of the secrets of happiness and cohesiveness. It's the opposite of selfishness.

It reminds me of a catch-phrase Frank often repeated: "If you want to be happy, think what you can do for someone else. If you'd like to be miserable, think about what's owed to you."

I've seen with the Hendersons, the Perdues, and countless other families that the rewards for being philanthropic are almost endless. They include:

- The good feelings you get from know you're making a positive difference in people's lives.

- Having a good name,

- Having influence

- Receiving societal approval

But most of all, behaving philanthropically is one of the

best sources of "family glue". Philanthropy can be the connective tissue that binds family members together across the generations.

Behaving philanthropically tells family members, "This is who we are! This is what we believe in! This is how we do things!"

Members from all generations can be a part of this. It's also especially valuable for engaging both family members who work in the company and those who don't.

Take advantage of this wonderful activity. The rewards for family cohesion are priceless.

Checklist for Possible Philanthropic Activities

> **For the older family members, instead of exchanging gifts with each other, give gifts to those in need.**
> The Perdues regularly pack Christmas gifts at Thanksgiving to give to Reservists who are serving overseas, or to associates who've experienced flooding, fires, or other disasters. We write letters to the individuals to accompany the gifts and the younger family members participate by coloring holiday decorations that we include in the packages.
>
> **Contact your any local charity such as Habitat for Humanity.**
> See if they'd like the services of your family. If you choose Habitat, the family could help in constructing or repairing a home. You don't need building skills; you'll be told how you can help

and you'll be given directions for doing it.

Model philanthropic behavior.
Have family members collect their no-longer-
needed clothing and bring them to a homeless
shelter or a shelter for abused women. In the
process, the youngsters will learn that caring for
others is part of the family's values.

**If your family can, you might want to create a
family foundation.**
Both the Hendersons and the Perdues do this, and
it's a wonderful tool for having family members
come together for something that does good,
that's bigger than any individual, and that's
designed to continue across the generations.

CHAPTER 5

Money and Happiness:
David Copperfield's Brilliant Advice

Frank Perdue was a big believer in the *David Copperfield Secret of Happiness.*

We're not talking about my favorite magician; we're talking about the novel by Charles Dickens.

In the novel *David Copperfield*, Wilkins Micawber proclaimed that if you spend less than your income you'll be happy. If you spend more, you'll be miserable.

You know what level of spending makes you happy, and you probably have figured out just how frugal you want your children or their children to be. Still, I can tell you that Frank Perdue was to the core a frugal man, and he liked it that way.

I'm even ready to guess that he took at least as much pleasure in living below his means as others might take in living a lavish lifestyle. He always lived astonishingly below his income.

Our home, for example, was a comfortable ranch house with neighbors that included retired teachers and a guy who ran a grain elevator. Trust me, millionaire's row it was not.

I have a favorite memory of this. One day in the late 1990s, Owen Schweers, the Perdue Director of Packaging, was bringing an important businessman to meet Frank at our Salisbury home. As Schweers pulled up beside our house, his VIP passenger started laughing heartily.

"Okay, that's a good one!" he chortled. "But you're not going to get me on this. I know Frank Perdue wouldn't live in that little ranch house!"

Schweers stopped his car near our front door. "But it is Frank's house," Schweers insisted.

"Sure, *right*," said the VIP, still guffawing.

Suddenly his laughter stopped because there was Frank, opening the door and stepping outside to greet his guests.

"Oh my God," whispered the VIP to Schweers, "Frank really does live here!"

Living in an unpretentious house was typical of Frank. He had no interest in a McMansion, and most status symbols left him cold.

As an example, when we travelled, which we did a lot while visiting overseas buyers, we could have used a chauffeur-driven limousine in whatever city we were in. Instead Frank used the local subway system.
This happened whether it was New York, London, Moscow, Tokyo, or Beijing. He preferred being with average people, that is, people who use public transportation. His ego didn't require a limousine.

Once in 1995, we spent six weeks driving form Maryland to California and back. Where did he, the head of Perdue Farms, and I, a Sheraton heiress stay? Motel 6, every night. We did it because this chain was clean, always friendly, and the check-in procedures were wonderfully rapid.

Something else: I bet I had the highest cobbler bill in Maryland because Frank didn't throw out his shoes. Instead we had them repaired. Similarly, I'm also guessing that we might have had one of the highest re-weaving bills in New York.

Because he was a representative of his brand, he made sure to dress well and bought from the top designers. But he made them last. If the elbow of an Emiglio Zegna suit was wearing thin, I'd quick send it to Alice Zotta, a New York reweaver, for repairs. This happened lots.

Frank continuously encouraged his kids in this kind of thinking. As he told his children in one of the family newsletters in which he was encouraging them to live below their means: "It's not fun to be worried about whether you can pay your bills."

Frank was frugal, and the money he didn't spend generally went to philanthropy. He felt a deeper and more lasting pleasure supporting, for instance, United Way, than spending money on himself.

He really did live the David Copperfield message of spending less than his income. But he put what he didn't spend to good use, supporting the charities that he loved.

Could avoiding status-type spending add to your happiness? Would the David Copperfield approach be right for you?

If it's important to you to live far enough beneath your means that you don't have to worry about money, what could you spend less on and still be happy?

Checklist for Being Frugal

Fly economy class.
Frank's attitude was you get there just as fast, so why pay more?

Use public transportation.
There's a benefit to this beyond money. Families of means are at risk of living in a bubble, and although this won't cure the bubble problem, using the subway and buses is a start. Besides, using public transportation is ecological. And on buses you'll meet people and hear stories you might never hear otherwise.

Live in a less expensive house than you can afford.
My own view is, investing in philanthropy yields a better pay-off in personal satisfaction than investing in ego.

Buy quality clothes, but make them last.
Cobblers and re-weavers for repairs can be a good investment when you have quality clothes. If you haven't ever used a re-weaver, you may find their results astonishing. When Alice Zotta had finished re-weaving a worn-through elbow or knee, I couldn't detect where she had done it. It was the equivalent of new.

CHAPTER 6

New Family Members: Welcome, Embrace, and Celebrate Them!

Being an in-law in a family business has many more complexities than joining a non-business family. For starters, in-laws probably see a lot more of the other family members when they're joined together in a family business.

And of tremendous importance, if there's a serious family quarrel, it impacts not just family members, it can ripple through the company and then through all the company's stakeholders such as suppliers, lenders, and if the company is a large one, it can impact the tax base of the community.

In view of the extreme importance of family harmony in a business family, it's important that every new member feel welcomed and part of the family. Disasters happen when family cultures fail to blend following a marriage.

On the other hand, it can be exceptionally gratifying when it goes well. I once asked a grandson-in-law how he felt about being a member of such an all-encompassing family.

To my undying delight, Keith Eliason, who had been a married-in for more than 20 years when I asked this question, answered, "I never felt that I wasn't a part of the family." He went on to say that "Since the beginning, being members of the family is simply who we all are."

Since not all families have Eliason's experience, and since families don't automatically blend, what are some things that families can do to make it easier?

Things Successful Families Do to Welcome New Members:

- **Newsletters:** Whenever someone gets engaged, the Perdues have a family newsletter interviewing the soon-to-be new member. In this newsletter, we learn not just about the engagement and what the proposal was like, but also about what's important to the individual including their hobbies, pastimes, career aspirations and anything that we can learn to help us reach out to and embrace the new family member.

- **A Family Gift:** The Perdues give a new bride a silver necklace with a large silver coin pendant. At family occasions, we all wear our silver coins, and this is yet another way of showing that she's now part of us. In our case, the coin is part of our history because it's a coin from the sunken treasure ship, the Atocha, and the coins are in the family because Frank Perdue was one of the financial backers for finding the Atocha. Your family gift will be different, but if you can find something meaningful, start a tradition of something that says, "Now you're one of us."

- **Wedding Re-enactment:** The Hendersons re-enact all the weddings that happened in the year preceding that year's family reunion. Because the Hendersons are a large and geographically dispersed family, it's guaranteed that some family members will have missed a wedding that's in a different part of the country or even in a different country entirely.

At the annual reunion with its wedding reenactment, the bride gets to wear her wedding dress, and her attendants are the youngest children, usually ages three to ten. We have bridesmaids costumes for the little girls. The bride gets to walk down an "aisle" in the ballroom of our family home in New Hampshire, and she does it to the same music she used for her real wedding.

Her husband is waiting for her, dressed in a suit or a tux, or whatever he wore for the real wedding earlier that year. He's attended by young groomsmen who are also ages three to ten. A member of an older generation, (in our case, Dr. Zé Ayala) invites the newlyweds to repeat the vows that they said in their real wedding.

It's a surprisingly emotional event and deeply meaningful for family members who couldn't attend the real ceremony. Also, I've had our re-enactment brides tell me that during the re-enactment, they feel the same nervousness and happiness as they did during their real weddings. And they talk about the re-enactments for years afterwards. It's an amazing "welcome to the family."

The re-enactments always end on a lighter note, with Dr. Ayala stating, "And now, by the powers *not invested in me by anyone*, I pronounce you legally married five months ago!" (or whatever the actual timing was.)

There's a reception afterwards with toasts, and in some cases, the "welcome to the family" toasts given at the real wedding are repeated. It's just a joyous tradition and so respectful of the older members in their 80s or 90s who couldn't attend the real wedding.

- **Give a *What It Means to Be Us* book.**

  The Hendersons give the newly married-in a copy of our hardcover book with photographs of the family members, essays on who we are, and birthdays of the family members. See page 76 for the ideas on creating your own *What It Means to Be Us* book.

- **The Whole Family Sends Birthday Cards.**

  One recently engaged and soon-to-be Perdue family member told me, what a wonder and delight it was for her, that on her birthday every family member sent her a happy birthday message. In one case, two 4- and 6-year-old cousins made a video wishing her happy birthday. She said this gesture felt unimaginably welcoming.

- **Inclusion in Family Costumes.**

  This same young woman was delighted when her future mother-in-law included her in Halloween costumes so that three generations dressed in identical Wonder Woman costumes. "It made a huge impression," the young woman told me. "It's easy to see someone as an outsider, but they made the effort early on to treat me as one of their own."

HOW TO MAKE YOUR FAMILY BUSINESS LAST

- **Country-of-Origin Flags:**

  This probably applies to very few families, but it's highly effective. In the case of the Hendersons, we have in-laws from Japan, Holland, Honduras, China, and Korea. In addition, we have first generation Italian, Spanish, and Canadian members. At family reunions, we hang flags from everyone's country on the porch where we have evening cocktails. Family members from other countries tell me it means the world to them to have their new family honor and respect their country of origin.

- **College Flags:**

  If it's a newly-engaged or newly married couple, make them feel welcome by displaying the college flag or flags of the couple. In the grand scheme of things, this is a small gesture, but still, it's a symbolic way of showing respect for who they are. Anything that shows respect for their background can go a long way in starting things off right.

- **A Now-You're-One-of Us Welcome Kit:**

  The welcome kit can start with a history of the business. If appropriate, include samples of what the business makes. (The qualification "appropriate" is material here. I went to school with a girl whose family business was sanitary napkins. When I think of her, I feel safe saying that not all family businesses have samples that would be just right for a welcome-to-the-family gift.)

40

- **A Booklet with a Photograph of Each Family Member.**

  This can include a couple of sentences about each family member, to help the new member get his or her bearing.

Checklist for Welcoming New Family Members

Newsletters

A Sentimental Gift that all new family members receive

Wedding Re-enactment

Gift of a *What It Means to Be Us* book

Birthday or engagement cards from the whole family

County of origin flags at family get-togethers

College flags at family get-togethers

A Now-You're-One-Of Us Welcome Kit:

Resources:

Costumes: If your family chooses to do wedding re-enactments in the cases where not all family members could attend a faraway wedding, it adds enormously to the festivities if there are young family members, say 2 to 10, who can be attendants. Get them fun costumes from Amazon.com. Amazon has a large choice of wedding attendant costumes for boys and girls.

HOW TO MAKE YOUR FAMILY BUSINESS LAST

Flags: If you have family members from other countries, you can use your printer for printing their countries' flags from images on the Internet. You can also buy flags on Amazon, or even better, to the Flag Store, http://www.flagstore.com. You'll find there an array of flags to honor in-laws, such as if they served in the Armed Forces, display the flag of their branch of the service, or maybe the college they attended.

Publisher or InDesign: If you're up for it, including learning and using the publishing program, Publisher (if you're a PC person) or InDesign (if you're a Mac person), then make a booklet with the names and photographs of family members. It will be a much-appreciated gift for the new family member, and it's also a relatively easy project if you want to learn a publishing program. Becoming proficient in a publishing program is a huge advantage for communicating with your family. Or if you have a family office, maybe someone there could take on this project.

CHAPTER 7

Service to the Family Award:
Bypass the "Gimmes"

Have you ever thought of the purpose of awards? Surprisingly, the part that's visible when the recipient accepts the plaque or trophy is probably less than 10% of the real impact of awards.

The other 90% is that awards are about shaping our values and making us aware of what our group admires. They have a deep impact on an organization's culture. Most of all, awards are about focusing attention on behavior that we want to encourage.

Foster an Attitude of Giving Back Rather Than Taking

Years ago, when I was developing the Service to the Family Award for both my families, my goal was to foster a variant of President Kennedy's famous slogan, "Ask not what your country can do for you, ask what you can do for your country."

For a family to survive and thrive across the generations, members need to be thinking of what they can do for their families. The problem is, we all know of families where the focus was the more selfish one of, "What can I get?"

Members with the "What can I get?" kind of attitude often ended up in lawsuits. And once they've chosen to go down that road, the family relationships virtually never recover.

For those individuals, in the effort to get more of their share, they lost not only the money that went to the lawyers, they also ruptured some of the most important relationships in their lives. They destroyed what can bring joy and meaning to their lives for the purpose of getting something totally superfluous: more money.

I wish I could tell you how often I've seen this happen. And it's not just sad, it's tragic.

How much misery those families would have avoided if members had learned from their earliest years that family is about looking out for the good of the whole; membership means reciprocal obligations; being a part of a family means giving back, not just taking.

I designed the Service to the Family Award to encourage family members to focus on giving back. It was almost a guarantee to have people understand that "What it means to be us" includes service to the greater good, in this case, as the name implies, serving the family.

If you'd like to develop an award designed to foster feeling of giving back, here's a checklist on how to do it.

Checklist for a Service to the Family Award

> **Decide what kind of behaviors you'd like to encourage.**
> In the case of the two families I'm closest to, it was anything that made the family closer, more high-functioning, and more a source of pride or inspiration to our members and to the community.

Name the Award.
In our case, it's the Service to the Family Award.

Decide what goes along with the award.
You could have a cash award, but I don't recommend it. Recognition and honor are what your award is truly about and money may cheapen it. Our awards consist of the 11 by 13" coffee table book about our family, *What It Means to Be Us*. It's updated each year using print-on-demand technology. (In case your family would like to make a What It Means to Be Us book, see page 79 on Checklist for Writing Your Family's Book). The cover has on it, for example, "James Osborne, Winner; of the 2017 Service to the Family Award." Your awards may be something entirely different, such as a plaque or engraved cup or having the person's name inscribed on an honor roll wall.

Decide who the judges will be.
When our award began years ago, Augusta Petrone (she's the Henderson family matriarch) and I simply decreed who we thought had done most for the family. The next year, we invited nominations and Augusta and I plus the most recent winner voted on who it would be. After the third year, Augusta and I bowed out and the previous award winners became the judges from then on. After we got to seven, the first winner gets dropped as a judge so there's a steady state of seven judges.

Set up a timetable.
Decide when nominations are due; when the judging is complete; if the award needs to be

engraved or printed; and the date by which the final text is needed so it can be sent to the printer or engraver in time for the award ceremony.

Plan the ceremony that accompanies the award.

In the Henderson Family, it's given out at the end of a Saturday night dinner that's been going on for 127 years. There's a beautiful speech--culled from the nomination letters-on why the person won it and why the whole family is honored by what the winner did. The person who gives the speech is last year's winner Also, read the names of the previous winners. Have toasts in honor of the new winner and after that, toasts in honor of the past winners.

Resources:

If you choose a coffee table book with photos from the family and the winner's name on the cover, PrestoPhoto does a good job. https://www.prestophoto.com/create/iphoto-aperture-book-printing.

CHAPTER 8

Codify Your Values: Create an Ethical Will

One of the most meaningful and moving things Frank Perdue did for his family is something that you can do for yours: he didn't just leave them material things; he also "willed" them his values.

What is an "ethical will"?

An ethical will puts in writing the values that the head of the family believes will help his or her descendants to lead happy and productive lives. Ideally, it becomes part of the family's culture, and when the children and their children are looking for meaning and identity, an ethical will lets them know, that "This is the kind of people we are."

By the way, ethical wills are not something new; they've existed since Biblical times. I suggested that Frank use this ancient practice to help make sure his ideas were codified and could be passed down to future generations.

Leave Your Family Something More Important Than Money

Frank's ethical will was something of a joint venture for us. He was receptive to the idea because, by the time he was in his 80s, he had come to believe that people with integrity, that is, people who follow their highest values, will at the end of the day lead happier lives. These people gain self-respect, people trust them, and they have successful relationships not just with others, but with themselves.

47

Although Frank believed strongly in the importance of values, both of us had observed that an inheritance can short-circuit this process. There was a phrase we both related to: "Adversity breeds character. Prosperity breeds monsters." Frank wanted to help guarantee that the values he cherished were front and center in the family's culture.

You've probably observed, as we did when observing the children of other families of means, that over and over again, wealth without values leads to unhappiness. It can make children vulnerable to destructive behaviors such as, for example, substance abuse. Lack of values can turn heirs into playboys and can accelerate the arc of "shirtsleeves to shirtsleeves in three generations."

By the way, Frank's focus on values didn't come out of the blue. Frank and his first wife, Madeline, had been working to instill good values in their children from birth. However, in his 80s Frank was ready to embrace the idea of embedding the values in the family culture so these values would still exist after his passing.

He and I spent three days on the project. Frank would dictate his ideas, I'd type them, we'd discuss them, and then I'd type his changes. By the end of the process, there wasn't a single word that Frank hadn't put his heart into; he gave it the seriousness it deserved.

At his funeral, each grandchild read one of the parts of it. In the time since, every family member including new members through marriage, received a framed copy of this. Many of them keep Frank's ethical will on their desks and others keep it on a bedside table. I often hear family members referring to it, including buttressing an argument or a position by referring to it. It really is part of our culture.

Frank's Ethical Will

1. Be honest always.

2. Be a person whom others are justified in trusting.

3. If you say you will do something, do it.

4. You don't have to be the best, but you should be the best you can be.

5. Treat all people with courtesy and respect, no exceptions.

6. Remember that the way to be happy is to think of what you can do for others. The way to be miserable is to think about what people should be doing for you.

7. Be part of something bigger than your own self. That something can be family, pursuit of knowledge, the environment, or whatever you choose.

8. Remember that hard work is satisfying and fulfilling.

9. Nurture the ability to laugh and have fun.

10. Have respect for those who have gone before and learn from their weaknesses and build on their strengths.

Checklist for Creating Your Ethical Will
    Analyze the values that work in your family

HOW TO MAKE YOUR FAMILY BUSINESS LAST

List them.

Brainstorm as many as you can.

You may find that the ones that weren't immediately obvious turn out to be the most valuable, so stretch to find more.

Cut your list down to ten or fewer.
A longer list risks losing impact.

Try it out on some of your family members.
They may have insights that are invisible to you.

Think about it for a few days and then revise it.

Plan how you'll use it.
Will it be read at your funeral? Do you want family members to have it now? Do you want to have copies engraved on a copper plate, which is given to each family member, signaling the importance of the document? Would you like to have it read at family reunions? Will it be available to non-family members?

Writing an ethical will can be a priceless gift to your family. It may be one of your most cherished and meaningful gifts.

After all, the size of the family business is not what makes family members happiest. Their deepest and most enduring happiness will come from loving relationships with those they're closest to. Don't let your family leave this process to chance. Provide your family with the values that make these kinds of relationships possible. Do it now! It's never too early, and never too late.

CHAPTER 9

We Are the Stories We Tell Ourselves: So Tell the Stories!

Stories are what bind us together. Stories makes us stronger and more resilient. They make us think "us" rather than "me."

Why Do Stories Have So Much Impact?

If I were to give you 10 statistics right now, chances are tomorrow, you might not remember even one of them. But when your mother told you a story, there's a good chance that you could remember that story for a lifetime.

That's because our brains are wired to process and remember stories. Statistics? Not so much.

Stories are so important because, as brain scientists have shown, stories teach us to make sense of the world. Stories tell us who we are and where we fit in. Stories provide role models to guide us in such things as developing resilience or a sense of right and wrong. They're the bedrock of our family culture.

According to Dr. Robyn Fivush, Director of the Family Narratives Lab at Emory University, an overwhelmingly important part of successful child-rearing is having family members share their family stories. Members of families who know their family stories are more resilient, they're better off both physically and psychologically, they do better academically, and they're more satisfied with life.

HOW TO MAKE YOUR FAMILY BUSINESS LAST

When children know their family stories, it means they've spent time with their families. Maybe they learned the stories over dinner or during car trips or vacations. Families that spend time together and share their family stories, are likely to be high-functioning families.

Would you like a quick check up on how well your family is doing? See how many "yes" answers the young members of your family have for the following questions. If they have a lot of yes answers, it shows that they've spent a lot of quality time with you, and you've given them a good start in life.

Checklist for Knowing Your Family Narrative

This comes from Emory University Family Narrative Lab's "Do You Know Scale"

>   Do you know how your parents met?
>
>   Do you know where your mother grew up?
>
>   Do you know where your father grew up?
>
>   Do you know where some of your grandparents grew up?
>
>   Do you know where some of your grandparents met?
>
>   Do you know where your parents were married?
>
>   Do you know what went on when you were being born?

HOW TO MAKE YOUR FAMILY BUSINESS LAST

Do you know the source of your name?

Do you know some things about what happened when your brothers or sisters were being born?

Do you know which person in your family you look most like?

Do you know which person in the family you act most like?

Do you know some of the illnesses and injuries that your parents experienced when they were younger?

Do you know some of the lessons that your parents learned from good or bad experiences?

Do you know some things that happened to your mom or dad when they were in school?

Do you know the national background of your family (such as English, German, Russian, Chinese, and so on)?

Do you know some of the jobs that your parents had when they were young?

Do you know some awards that your parents received when they were young?

Do you know the names of the schools that your mom went to?

Do you know the names of the schools that your dad went to?

Do you know about a relative whose face "froze" in a grumpy position because he or she did not smile enough?

If there aren't a lot of "yes" answers, then spend more time with your children. Talk with them. Tell them the family stories. Read them the family newsletters you'll find in *How to Use Children's Newsletters to Strengthen Your Family's Culture.* Do the accompanying activities with them. You can find it on Amazon by me, Mitzi Perdue.

You'll improve their chances of doing well in life. And there's not much that matters as much as that.

Resource:

Robyn Fivush,
http://www.psychology.emory.edu/cognition/fivush/lab/FivushLabWebsite/index.html

CHAPTER 10

Write or Record the Family's History: Memories Are What Make Us into Us

Imagine something terrible for a moment. If you lost your memory, as in Alzheimer's, you would have lost one of the most basic factors that makes you *you.* Without memory, you'd have trouble making good decisions; you'd no longer have a foundation for judging what works and what's important. Further, you wouldn't make a lot of effort to protect things that ought to be important in your life because you'd no longer know why they're important. Worse, you wouldn't even know that they're important at all.

Well, no need to keep imagining. I can promise that the fact that you're reading this means you haven't lost your memory, and you really are you.

Do Family Members Know the Family's History?

But what about your family's memory? Can we be as sure that your family's memory of where they come from is a healthy and intact as your own memory?

How much does your extended family remember where the family business came from, what made it what it is today, and what sacrifices, efforts and tenacity went into making this wonderful family business you have today? Even if current family members know these stories, will future members of the family know them?

A family history in the form of a book can play a

powerful role in helping family members understand where they came from and what's important. Both the Hendersons and the Perdues follow the strategy of having family history books.

In the Henderson family, we have five generations of family books, and it's a family rule that when you're over 60, you are supposed to write a book of memoirs. Having books that let us know where we came from is among the strongest factors in keeping the Hendersons together since 1890.

It's the same with the Perdues. We're a fourth-generation family business, and the books started with the first generation, Mr. Arthur.

Having a family history is so important to a family's continuation that maybe it's not so much a question of whether to write a book, but rather, how to go about it.

Checklist for Ways to Have a Family History Written

If you're able, write the family history yourself; If you're brave enough to do it, see pages 229-237, for suggestions on how to do it.

Offer to pay a family member. Is there an English major whom you could pay to do it? Maybe someone at home with young children?

Hire someone from the local university.

Hire someone from the Internet. There are many services that will do this. UpWork.com has many people who can help with this, and you can find a range of prices and experience on offer.

HOW TO MAKE YOUR FAMILY BUSINESS LAST

What If No One Wants to Write the Family History?

There is another approach if the family doesn't want a family history book: hire a knowledgeable videographer to interview family members.

"You can communicate that family history as video," says videographer Andrew Suhl. "Kids watch video on their computers, watches, and soon their driverless cars. This is how people will consume this information in the future."

What It's Like To Be Part of a Video

If Suhl were videotaping you, his goal would be to have a relaxed conversation.

"I find that within 10 minutes of an interview, the person forgets about the camera and the lights. We're just having a talk. Instead of speechifying, the interaction becomes relaxed and having fun."

Suhl would ask you about some of your greatest challenges and greatest victories, and he'd ask you about growing up, what life was like at the time, and what was important to you.

If you grew up in the 1930s, he might ask you about the coal man and the ice man. He'd also try to illustrate your story, including old photos, passports, newspaper clippings, and anything else to illustrate the story.

"We can hire archival researchers to get material," he points out. "There are people who specialize in this kind of thing. We can find experts who can do research in almost any language or find newsreels or discover unexpected artifacts that are both illuminating and surprising in how they reveal the individual's life."

Adding historical context deepens the viewers emotional connection to the story. Typically, the grandkids will find these stories fascinating. They'll value these stories, and they'll be shaped by then.

Having a video portrait of a family is a way to pass on the family values from one generation to the next. In truth, having a story from an elder passed on to the younger generations is how it's always been done. It's ancient as cave man days. Suhl is just bringing technology to bear on that ancient need.

Book Resources:

Gary W. Clark, Write a Captivating Family History: Don't Bore Your History to Death – Add Context to the Story. May 26, 2015.
This is a tremendous resource for information on how to write your family history and how to add historical information to put it in context.

Katie Wiebe *How to Write Your Personal or Family History*: (If You Don't Do It, Who Will?)
 Feb 7, 2017 by Katie Funk Wiebe helps beginning memoir writers get started collecting the stories of their lives. She gives hints for recalling distant memories and tracking down family heirlooms.

Association of Personal Historians.org. I haven't used them, but it is a resource that's out there.

HOW TO MAKE YOUR FAMILY BUSINESS LAST

Video Resources:

Your local college, university, or community college is likely to have someone who is skilled in videography and storytelling. Or try UpWork.com.

Or Contact Andrew Suhl, Family Voices Media. You can phone him at: 914 405 0776 or e-mail him at: asuhl@familyvoicesmedia.com. His website is www.voicesmedia.com.

CHAPTER 11

Develop And Maintain Your Family Archive

Why bother to keep your family's important records?

This is really the same issue we discussed in the previous chapter, the one about writing a book or creating a video record. Not keeping records is like consigning your family's legacy to a memory-robbing disease.

As with Alzheimer's, if a family can't remember its past, it's hard to make sense of the present and difficult to plan the future.

The records from an archive let family members know that they're part of something bigger than themselves and that the world didn't start with them. It also lets them know that family members before them faced hardships and got through them.

In short, an archive creates a lasting family legacy. It will be a blessing for generations to come.

What Do You Put in a Family Archive?

Your family's archive can contain materials such as unpublished and one-of-a-kind items, but it also might contain newspaper accounts and in some cases, books written by family members. It will likely include memorabilia and objects such as embroideries or quilts or scrapbooks. It can be the backbone of maintaining the family's culture because it tells "Where we came from" and "What it means to be us."

It also can mean a connection with those who have gone before. In the Perdue archive, there's a valentine someone from Frank's 3rd grade class sent him. Somehow, it's unreasonably moving to have something tangible from a relative's life that shows that he or she was once a kid. It's a connection his relatives wouldn't have had otherwise.

Or just recently I heard from a widower who lost his wife of 62 years. He told me that reading her diaries almost brings her back when he's reading them. The moments those documents give him are beyond all price.

Backup Stories with Documents and Memorabilia

Documents and mementos are priceless, but in addition to objects, some of what will be part of your family's legacy will be the stories the family tells. It's critical to have the stories backed up by records.

It's the same principal as the game that we've all played as children. I knew it as "Whisper down the Lane," although you may know it as "Telephone," "Russian Scandal," "Chinese Whispers," or "Operator."

The essence of the game is, one person whispers something to the person sitting next to him who whispers it to the next person, and by the time ten or so people have heard the message, the last version has almost nothing to do with the original. I remember when I played it in 4th grade, "Fifty-nine dollars," turned into "Fifty iron collars."

The game is proof of the old Chinese proverb that, "The faintest ink is stronger than the most powerful memory."

Because stories get garbled over time, or they get forgotten entirely, archives are an essential part of your family's culture and identity. You can hardly imagine how much you need an archive if your goal is to have the family last across the generations.

Checklist for creating an Archive
    Appoint an archivist.
    Someone needs to oversee this. In the families I'm closest to, being the Family Archivist, that is, the person in charge of the family's memories, is a high-prestige position. The Henderson Family Archivist, Roberta Henderson, is so esteemed for her work that she's twice won our Service to the Family Award. Among other things she's done is digitized 10,000 family records. By the way, being the Family Archivist is a great way for an individual who isn't working in the family business to make an important (very important) contribution to the family.

    Plan how to collect and track the information.
    This can be done on a spreadsheet, but using a professional relational database management program such as Filemaker Pro for Mac users and Access for PC users can be a worthwhile effort. Is there someone in the family who has a flair for computers and could set up a database that another family member could maintain? Or is there someone in the family office or even the family business who could set up an archive database?

    Use Denise Levenick's Three, Two, One rule for making backups.
    See more about her in the Resources section below. According to Levenick, you need three copies of digital media, including one on your computer, one on an external hard drive and one in the Cloud.

There should also be two paper copies, one of which is off-site. And finally, there's one original, where you keep wherever you have your archives. If it's a document, you really do want a paper copy. Paper or parchment can last thousands of years. The digital files you have right now could be inaccessible in a decade. I hope that's not true, but the possibility of their being inaccessible because of new formats is worth considering.

Avoid transparent tape, plain glue and metal staples.
These can leave stains and residue on your archival documents. I've seen them do their nasty work in as little as ten years.

Have your documents where mice or other rodents can't get at them.
This ought to be too obvious to mention, but oh well, here goes: It's so disconcerting to see, as I've seen, a letter from your great grandfather "decorated" by a mouse. I'm guessing that the odds of this happening to you are small, especially if you live in a big city in a high-rise apartment. But if you're in the country and it's a farm house…well, as I've said, I've seen it happen.

Checklist of Items to Archive
Artwork such as paintings or sketches

Awards

Books authored by family members

Collections like–who knows? –toy soldiers, sports memorabilia. If it's something that would give future family members an insight into what made a founder or someone in the business tick, include it.

Diaries

Diplomas

Genealogical information such as birth, marriage, and death certificates.

Genealogical research

Letters (These can be highly evocative. We can almost feel and see the ancestor's presence in their handwriting.)

Medical history. This is a little tricky because of privacy issues, but if you can manage it, this can be a gift to future generations in understanding those who came before, and possibly dealing with health issues that they may face.

Memberships in for instance, clubs, professional societies, fraternal organizations, honor societies.

Military records, such as discharge papers, honors.

Newspaper clippings

Notes on important business decisions. (The Perdue Archives has hundreds of pages of notes from Frank when he was deciding how to get into advertising. Without these notes, future generations might have no idea of the effort and focus Frank put into being the first to advertise a commodity.)

Photographs. Be sure to record who is in it and the date and location if known and, also if known the dates of birth and death of those in it. Record this information even for current photos because otherwise a generation from now, people won't know who is who.

Policy Statements

Reports

Scrapbooks

Textiles such as quilts, embroideries or needle point. If you know who made them and when, their value increases exponentially. (In the early 1900, my grandmother made some needlepoint chairs and it almost brings her back as I realize that she made each of those stitches. My sister taped a note to the bottom of each chair and the notes say who made the needlepoint seats and when. Those notes transform the chairs from merely being old to being amazing heirlooms,)

Company Documents to Consider Keeping

Your family business almost certainly won't need all the documents listed here. My two families only use about 75% of them, but I'm aware of families who use most of them.

This list probably isn't complete. If you think of documents that I should add to this list and that others might benefit from, please let me know. I'll add your idea or ideas to the list that follows and give you credit.

HOW TO MAKE YOUR FAMILY BUSINESS LAST

Just e-mail me at: Mitzi@MitziPerdue.com. I'd look on it as a public service if you would let me know because I'd like this chapter to be as useful as possible.

Maybe now's the time to share something with you. I only printed a few copies of this book with the idea that when people have suggestions for making this book more useful, I can quickly incorporate their recommendations and add them to the next printing. I share my dear late husband's view that "None of is as smart as all of us."

So please help me make this chapter better in the editions that follow. Besides, I'd love to hear from you.

Checklist of Company Documents

Advance Directive

Agreements on how, when and why loans can be made. https://www.entrepreneur.com/article/241295 Buy sell agreement https://www.entrepreneur.com/article/241295'

Archives Contents (Description written by archivist of what's in the archives.)

Assets

Corporate Governance

Digital Passwords in Case of Death or Disability.

Directory of Family Members and Key Company Officials

Estate and Trust Documents

HOW TO MAKE YOUR FAMILY BUSINESS LAST

Ethical Will

Family Code of Conduct

Family Constitution

Family Council Document

Family Education Goals

Family Employee Policy

Family Genealogy Documents

Family History Documents

Family Mission Statement

Foundation, the Letter of Donor Intent

Foundation Mission

Guardianship for Children

Last Will and Testament

Letters from the Grave to Descendants

Medical Treatment Authorization for a Minor

Ownership Agreement (Does stock go only to family members who are in the business, or does it go to bloodlines or can in-laws own stock?)

Power of Attorney, Financial

Power of Attorney, Medical

Stockholder Meetings Records

Trustees List

Trust Documents

Vacation Homes Rules and Directions

Voting Results Agreement: (Which decisions are consensus, which are 3/4 majority, which are simple majority.)

Voting Rights Agreement (i.e. Which decisions are made by bloodlines alone and which by in-laws as well)

Resources:

Denise Levenick is the authority I most respect. Her website, The Family Curator http://thefamilycurator.com, has vast amounts of information, including such things as how to fireproof your archives, how to digitize them, how to organize them and much more.

She's available for professional consulting and she also has written several books that can be useful to you. They're available on Amazon.com.

How to Organize Inherited Items: A Step-by-Step Guide for Dealing with Boxes of Your Parents' Stuff
How to Archive Family Keepsakes: Learn How to Preserve Family Photos, Memorabilia and Genealogy Records

CHAPTER 12

Compete for Family Business Prizes: You Win Just by Trying

If your family has the time and the inclination, competing for prizes and awards can have tremendous benefits.

- Working towards a common goal fosters teamwork.

- Trying to be the best means focusing on excellence.

- Competing for a prize is energizing and educational.

And if you win?

- The benefits to the brand can be enormous, including positive magazine, newspaper, television, and internet coverage.

- Third party accolades are more believable than advertising, and you can use these in your marketing,

- Pursuing and winning business and industry awards are key to increasing trust in your brand and products.

- Often the awards ceremonies are gala affairs and attending can be a perk for your employees and top clients.

- It's great for employee engagement. I know when Perdue won the LEED certification for being an environmental leader, it meant a lot to the Perdue associates.

- It's a great networking opportunity; you'll meet other energized and motivated people.

Competing for prizes makes me think of what Dr. Kimberly Kagan, a professor at West Point said about the value of people going all out to be the best that they can be: "Not doing your best means you're undercutting yourself. By not reaching your full potential, you're missing out on an experience that can be incredibly rewarding."

A Few of the Possible Prizes

- **National Small Business Awards.**
  These are, usually given out at the end of April or early May. The deadline is the beginning of January but, it's a good idea to start working on it several months ahead of time. The Awards include prizes for:
  - Small Business Person of the Year Award

  - Small Business Exporter of the Year

  - Phoenix Award for Small Business Disaster Recovery

  - Phoenix Award for Outstanding Contributions to Disaster Recovery - Public Official

  - Phoenix Award for Outstanding Contributions to Disaster Recovery - Volunteer

- Federal Procurement Award - Small Business Prime Contractor of the Year Award

- Federal Procurement Award - Small Business Subcontractor of the Year Award

- Federal Procurement Award - Dwight D. Eisenhower Award for Excellence

- 8(a) Graduate of the Year Award

- Small Business Development Center Excellence and Innovation Award

- Veterans Business Outreach Center Excellence in Service Award

- Women's Business Center of the Year Excellence Award

- Jody C. Raskind Lender of the Year

- Small Business Investment Company of the Year

- **The President's "E" and "E Star Awards.** The President's "E" Award was created by Executive Order of the President to afford suitable recognition to persons, firms, or organizations which contribute significantly in the effort to increase United States exports. Winners of the "E" and "E Star" Award are authorized to fly the blue and white banner, to display the accompanying certificate of commendation which is signed by the Secretary of Commerce in the name and by the authority of the President, to wear and issue to employees an "E" or "E Star" lapel pin, and to refer to the award in their advertising.

- **The Malcolm Baldrige National Quality Award.** This award is the highest level of national recognition for performance excellence that a U.S. organization can receive. The award focuses on performance in five key areas:
    - Product and process outcomes

    - Customer outcomes

    - Workforce outcomes

    - Leadership and governance outcomes

    - Financial and market outcomes

To receive the award, an organization must have a system that
    - Ensures continuous improvement in overall performance in delivering products and/or services
    - Provides an approach for satisfying and responding to customers and stakeholders

Global Family Business Award for Excellence in Family Business.

The award, which is regarded by many as the most prestigious distinction for successful family businesses, also serves as a platform for family businesses to exchange best practices and analyze the economic backdrop.

- **Excellence in Family Business Challenge,** Oregon State University, College of Business, Austin Family Business Program. This is for demonstrated excellence in one of three fundamental family business qualities: family harmony, generational development, or business renewal. All family businesses are eligible to apply regardless of size or longevity. A family business is broadly defined as having multiple family members or generations involved in the strategic direction, management, and/or working in the company with the intention for the business to remain in the family.

- **Family Firm Institute Awards.**
  Your family firm probably isn't eligible for the Family Firm Institute Awards since they're aimed at family business advisors and academics. Still, if you've been particularly pleased with your family business advisor, nominating him, her, or them would be a spectacular way of saying "Thank you!"

Checklist for Applying for Awards

Have I researched awards that my company might be eligible for? For instance, have I checked out my trade association's website, and done on-line searches?

Have I paid close attention to the application requirements, including the entry deadline?

Have I gathered the information for the application?

Have I answered the application questions precisely? The judges are hunting for ways to narrow down the field, and not following directions is an easy way to narrow them down.

Have I had others go over my application to help refine, focus and polish it?

Am I meeting the deadline for sending it in?

If I don't win, can I look at it as a learning experience and try again, and again?

Do I have the mental attitude that this isn't easy, but it's worth it?

Resources:

The Business Intelligence Group has a valuable free e-publication, *How to Win Business Awards and Influence Revenue.* https://www.bintelligence.com If you want to compete for awards, this 31page document is a must.

Startup Competition Guide: A Giant List of The Best Business Contests. For more information, go to http://grasshopper.com/blog/startup-competition-guide/ .

https://www.fundera.com/blog/best-small-business-awards This lists several dozen small business awards.

For the awards mentioned in the chapter:

National Small Business Awards
https://www.sba.gov/nsbw/awards

Malcolm Baldridge National Quality Award
https://www.nist.gov/baldrige/baldrige-award

Global Family Business Award

HOW TO MAKE YOUR FAMILY BUSINESS LAST

For more information go to:
http://www.globalfamilybusinessaward.com/about-the-award/

Excellence in Family Business Challenge
For more information, contact them at 1 800 859-7609 or
http://business.oregonstate.edu/familybusinessonline, and
navigate to the Excellence in Family Business Award.

Family Firm Institute Award
For more information go to
http://www.ffi.org/general/custom.asp?page=awards

CHAPTER 13

Family Glue: What It Means To Be Us

"Family glue" is a term we use a lot in the Henderson and Perdue families. It's shorthand for things that keep us close together as a family.

An example of a "gluey" activity for the Perdues is when we get together at Thanksgiving. Traditionally we spend some of the time wrapping holiday presents we've bought for disaster victims.

I love the concept of family glue, and I've often wondered if other families use the same term. In any case, I'm always on the lookout for activities that are gluey.

Just recently, I came across an idea which I now think of as one of the gluey-est ideas ever. I mentioned it in the "Family Traditions" chapter, the part about creating the book "What It Means to Be Us."

I think of creating this book is the *Ultimate Super Glue*. I highly recommend it for your family.

The idea is to ask family members "What does it mean to be us?"

For the Henderson Family, this resulted in a book of essays from family members. It's spectacular for bringing the family still closer.

Writing *What It Means to Be Us* means that all the family members spent time focusing on what we value as a family. It also means we know more about what makes each family member tick. It should be a wonderful resource for letting future generations know about those who came before them.

The idea for our "What It Means to Be Us" book comes from Linda Davis Taylor's book, *The Business of Family*. On page 27 of her book, Taylor asks a question that's so pivotal that when I read it, I carefully put a paperclip at that page, closed the book, and started thinking about it.

The question she suggested families consider is the one I've already mentioned, "What does it mean to be us?"

This question gets to the heart of everything we are as a family. It touches on our identity, our values, our culture, and maybe most importantly, just what it is that holds us together.

Before reading Taylor's question, I had never thought of, "What does it mean to be us?" I guess it's like a fish swimming in the ocean probably isn't aware that it's swimming in water. It's all around you and you take it for granted.

As I thought about "What does it mean to be us," I realized that I didn't have an immediate answer. And as I thought about it a bit more, it occurred to me that this isn't a question one person can answer. After all, Taylor didn't ask, "What does it mean to be *me*."

Yet I really wanted an answer. In my next Henderson family e-mail, I posed Taylor's question about what it means to be us. To my surprise and delight, I began getting back the most insightful and meaningful answers. They ranged from a few paragraphs words to many pages.

After the first ten or so answers, I noticed they had a common thread; people were grateful to be a part of the family, and being part of this family was one of the most important parts of their lives.

As more answers came in, I began forwarding them to the entire family. This had a snowball effect, because as family members read what other family members had written, they began wanting to add their views. Eventually, it got to the point where nobody wanted to be left out.

A Coffee Table Book Is Born

This lead to the idea of a coffee table style book, 11" by 13" that would have each person's essay, along with his or her birthday, photograph, and three or so adjectives describing the family.

But then, as long as we were going to have a book on *What It Means to Be Us*, why not include other design elements to make the resulting book as beautiful as possible?

The Henderson Clan has several tartans that could be background, plus I have hundreds of photographs of the family house that could likewise serve as a background. On top of that, with a little internet hunting, I found coats of arms for almost everyone, including reflecting their middle names or married names.

From there it made sense to add the family tree, so everyone could easily see who belonged to each branch.

Also, since we have a rule that by age 60, you're supposed to write an autobiography for future generations, we added a list of all the books we've written, and then added patents that family members received.

If you'd like to copy the phenomenally successful idea of having a *What It Means to Be Us Book* here are the steps:

Checklist for Creating a What It Means to Be Us Book

Appoint someone to oversee the project. That person is in charge of the following steps:

Contact all family members.
Send an e-mail to all your family members explaining that you'd like to create a "Book of Us" for future generations. Include all in-laws, and for that matter, anyone who's a "member" of the family such as close family friends or possibly people who've worked for the family for many years. Ask them to send you a brief essay of a couple of hundred words on what it means to be us. If you'd like to do what the Hendersons did, also ask for their birthdays, a photo, and three or more adjectives describing the family.

Describe your family in three adjectives.
If your families aren't the kind who would enjoy writing essays, an easier version of this is, ask for the photo and birthday, but be satisfied with three or more adjectives completing the sentence "Our family is….." For example, "Our family is kind, generous, and welcoming."

Set a deadline.
Choose one that will work for your family for
having the essay submitted. In the Henderson
family, the deadline was, "Have your essay in
within the next two weeks." Depending on how
your family operates, brace for the fact that many
won't be able to meet the deadline. With us, it
took from the end of December when I first read
Taylor's book to the end of March.

Have an alternate deadline.
It's highly likely that some of your family
members won't get their essays or their
adjectives in on time. The way around this, is
have either a family member or maybe someone
from the family office or an administrative
assistant for the family simply telephone people
asking them for either the adjectives or the essay.
Take down the information by phone, write it up,
and add it to your book.

Figure out the size of your book.
I recommend 11" by 13".

Design it.
Do you have some family member who's good
with design? I enjoy the program *InDesign* and
that's what I used. But if you don't have a family
member or know someone else who's a
designer, another possibility is going to
UpWork.com where you can post a request for a
designer.

**Find a printing company, probably on the
Internet.**

Upload your book.

Figure out how many copies you'd like and order them.
Have lots because you want all family members to have a copy, and you want some for future family members. I ordered 100.

Have a book party!
Celebrate for when you give the books to your family members. Make it an occasion!

Resources:

Linda Davis Taylor, *The Business of Family: How to Stay Rich for Generations* (June 30, 2015) It's available on Amazon.

There are many photobook internet companies, but I've used PrestoPhoto: https://www.prestophoto.com.

To find people who can help design this, look at UpWork. https://www.upwork.com

Or contact Jennifer Bumba, Graphic Designer, jenbumba@gmail.com. She designed the "What It Means to Be Us" book for the Hendersons. She's quick, imaginative, and fun to work with. She'll have ideas you hadn't thought of.

CHAPTER 14

Create An Education Committee: You Need One Even If You Don't Know You Need One!

How many family businesses have an education committee? It meets such an obvious need and yet, with the exception of the Hendersons and Perdues, I've not yet met another family that formalizes this very necessary function. I like having our Education Committee because I see it as a wonderful tool for enabling family members to be more knowledgeable about the company and to know more about the great legacy that they're part of.

An education committee can be a gift for your family, increasing their awareness of who they are and where they came from.

Advantages of an Education Committee

- The more the family members know about the family business, the better the family decisions and the deeper the attachment to the business.

- Having a common source of information is a unifying force.

- It's a chance to involve family members who aren't working in the business

- It's a chance to keep people up-to-date, not only on the family business, but also on current thinking on family businesses.

HOW TO MAKE YOUR FAMILY BUSINESS LAST

How It Works in the Perdue Family

Several years ago, when we were discussing forming an education committee, I sent an e-mail asking family members to rank what topics would interest them most. This is the list we voted on, although in the original they weren't in this order.

- **Learning people skills including basic etiquette**
  According to Cynthia Lett, an author and public speaker who focuses on these issues, "Eighty-five percent of business success is people skills, and a lot of these people skills depend on knowing how to say things in ways that don't cause resistance."

- **Knowing the basics of the family business,**
  For the Perdues, it is Chicken 101.

- **Knowing the family history**
  Knowing where we came from, and that it took effort and struggle to get to where we are today, increases our appreciation of the legacy we will be handing on to future generations.

- **Knowing the family's core values**
  Values such as honesty, integrity, teamwork, caring for others, and that family members are part of something bigger than the individual, and that the individual can't always have his or her way.

- **Knowing the importance of giving back.**

- **Teamwork and Trust-building skills**

- **Learning about finance, such as how to read a profit and loss**

- **Investing 101**

HOW TO MAKE YOUR FAMILY BUSINESS LAST

I had been hesitant even to include "etiquette skills" since that seemed somewhat "fluffy" compared to other possibilities, such as financial literacy or investing 101. However, this is by far the topic that got the most votes.

If you choose to form an education committee, what are the things it can do? I'm pretty sure you're not going to want to do all of them, but these are things that Whitney Van Der Hyde (Education Committee Vice Chair) and I do for our family:

How to Create an Education Committee

Begin by creating a vision statement for your committee. A vision statement provides clarity on what you're trying to do, and it states the goal or the end result.

In my family's case, the vision of the Family Education Committee is:

The Family continues across the generations as good stewards of both the family business and the family's legacy. Our goal is responsible stewardship, effective governance, and deep awareness and understanding of the family legacy.

To accomplish this mission, the Family Education Committee will provide learning tools and experiences for current and future generations: family newsletters for both adults and children, lectures, book reviews, participation in conferences, family vacations, active participation in the company's 100th Anniversary, contracts with family business counselors, and learning best practices from other family business owners.

HOW TO MAKE YOUR FAMILY BUSINESS LAST

Checklist of Activities

You probably won't do all of these ideas and you'll have some of your own, but this is what the Perdue Education Committee does:

> **In newsletters, we review books.**
> The books can be on management, family businesses, or governance. We help keep everyone up-to-date on the current thinking in the field of family businesses.
>
> **In newsletters, we interview company associates**.
> We get current information about what's going on in the company, including the processing facilities, farms, laboratories, and transportation facilities.
>
> **Have family newsletters for children**.
> These include information on family history and lore and values. They're unashamedly designed to strengthen the culture that keeps the family going.
>
> **Anniversary book**
> Does your company have a 21st, 25th, 50th, or more anniversary coming up? The Education Committee can work on its content. In our case, the Chicken 101 information, which comes from visiting plants and farms and talking with old timers, will be part of our 100th anniversary book.
>
> **Arrange site visits for the family.**
> Make sure family members see the company's operations. They can't know and feel attached to it if they never visit it.
>
> **Arrange site visits designed specifically for children.**

Our kids love a visit to the hatchery where they get to see the baby chicks hatch.

Arrange family vacations

Arrange lectures from family business gurus.

Arrange for reports when family members attend family business conferences.

Let family members know when there are family business conferences and other educational opportunities.
We make sure these opportunities don't just slip by with no one paying attention

Resources:

To find upcoming events, go to www.TrustedFamily.net and you'll find more than 100 family business

How to Strengthen Your Family Legacy with Newsletters Examples, Stories, Templates, Techniques, and Resources.
It's available on Amazon under Mitzi Perdue.

How to Use Children's Newsletters to Strengthen Your Family's Culture
Templates, Activities, Tips, Research, and Resources.
Available on Amazon under Mitzi Perdue

CHAPTER 15

Ways Frank Perdue Helped Embed the Culture in the Company

Frank was a big believer in the importance of a company's culture. He told me one day, and I wrote it in my diary, "Values are at the heart of a culture, and part of a leader's job includes creating the culture."

He was acutely aware of the importance of precedent and how every action a leader takes

In view of which, have you considered the precedent you create when you take an action? That what you do right now is also the way many things may be done in the future? This is true whether you work in the family business or not.

Frank Perdue had an almost uncanny awareness of precedent. Given how much else he had on his mind, I was endlessly impressed by how conscious he was of how any of his actions, whether large or small, would impact the family culture and the company culture.

I don't think he ever read life coach Martha Beck's saying that "How you do something is how you do everything," but he acted as if he had.

He was a big believer in the power of where a leader focuses his or her attention. "It's not what you expect, it's what you inspect," Frank used to say. In other words, what the leadership looks into and measures and watches out for are the things that reveal what the real values are.

He set precedents for both the business and the family. I've mentioned things we did for the family culture in previous chapters, but for the moment take a look at things he did for embedding the culture in the company.

Frank Monitored What He Cared About

- Do we insure a good product? He used to have employees buy competitors' products and then in blind tests at our facilities, measure how theirs stacked up against ours. I think the factors that we compared ourselves to other covered 38 categories. If we weren't on top, there would be changes in how we did things.

- Do we insist that people are treated well?

- Do we live up to our slogan: Quality, Service, Reliability?

- Do we monitor our environmental footprint?

- Do people get fired for ethical lapses?

Frank made sure that these were more than just slogans stored somewhere in a binder. In his life, he created tens of thousands of handwritten notes to different associates, checking up on these different factors.

If an individual didn't respond to one of these notes in a couple of days, he or she was in danger of a fate that must have seemed worse than death: *a Follow Up Call from his Executive Assistant, Elaine Barnes.* (Ah yes, a Terrifying Concept!) (Perdue associates have told me how much they *didn't* want to get one of these calls.)

HOW TO MAKE YOUR FAMILY BUSINESS LAST

Frank Showed People They Were Important to Him

That was the inspecting side of things. But he also put tremendous effort into showing people they were important to him.

That meant attending weddings and funerals and generally just being there for people. Years have gone by, but I still hear from people at how impressed they were when Frank would even charter a plane in order to be there for a parent's funeral.

When I was writing Frank's biography back in 2013, I was stunned by the number of Perdue associates who told me that when, for instance, a child was hospitalized, they'd get a phone call from Frank, asking what Frank could do to help. Sometimes this even meant Frank's calling medical friends at Johns Hopkins to see if something additional could be done.

I also know because I was part of it, that most weekends, Frank and I would be visiting Perdue associates who were in the hospital. He'd sit at their bedside, listen, share stories and memories, of when appropriate, tell jokes.

He even would call on retired associates; he had the attitude that they were still important to him even if they weren't getting a paycheck from him.

During Desert Storm, Frank used to write personal letters every month to the 82 Reservists who were deployed in Iraq. He'd even make a 10-hour round trip to drive to attend their homecomings.

HOW TO MAKE YOUR FAMILY BUSINESS LAST

Perdue has a strong culture, and it was planned, nurtured, encouraged, tested, and passed on, generation after generation.

Checklist for Things to Monitor:

Does our company pay attention to;

> How people are treated?
>
> Do we monitor such things as our environmental footprint?
>
> Diversity?
>
> Quality?
>
> Reliability?
>
> Service?
>
> Teamwork?
>
> Do we step in and help when disaster strikes?
>
> What do we do to show people who work for the company that they are important?
>
> Do we attend weddings?
>
> Do we attend Funerals?
>
> Do we visit the sick?
>
> Do we visit retired people?

Do we stay in contact if any of the employees are Reservists and deployed overseas?

How much do our actions carry out the mission statements and values we say we believe in?

Checklist of Things Frank Did That Created Loyalty

These are ways that family members both working and not working in the business can make a really important contribution.

Learn people's names, including the hourly workers.
When we were going through the chicken plants, Frank knew the names of thousands of the workers on the line, and when he'd introduce me to one of them, he'd tell me something personal about them, such as "Delsie has two sons in college," or "Norton has been with the company 32 years."

Be there for people outside of the work place.
We attended countless weddings and funerals, and frequently visited employees who were hospitalized. Frank showed his respect by taking the time to show that they were important.

Show retirees that they're still important.
On weekends, we would often drive to visit retired people in their homes. Former employees were still "part of the family," even though they were no longer receiving a paycheck.

Be supportive when employees have difficult family events.
When an associate lost a family member, Frank

would often drop everything to call the person and condole with him or her.

Encourage employees.
Perdue associates have told me that Frank had an uncanny sense of when one of them was having a tough time, even if they were many layers below him in management. When someone was having a discouraging day, often Frank would appear in the person's office, sit beside his or her desk, and ask what resources he could provide to help. Or maybe he'd just say a few encouraging words about believing in the person. He could transform a person's day.

The pay-off for having a strong company culture, one where workers, are willing to go-over-and-above for the company, can mean undreamed of success for you and your organization. Working on culture, whether for the family or the family business can be among the most important things you do.

CHAPTER 16

Choosing A Family Business Advisor

Part of both the Perdue and the Henderson Family's culture is, neither family is afraid to ask for help when it's needed. In the case of Frank, when he needed help, he simply went out and found it.

It was a mark of his intelligence that when he needed help with legal, or governmental affairs, or advertising, or family business issues, he spent the time and money to get that help. Once he had completed his research on who would be the best for the job, he hired the person or persons and listened to them.

This contrasts with members of family business who wait until problems become serious or even insurmountable. Frank was proactive.

If You Need Help, Get It.

Being proactive was how Frank conducted his life. He anticipated issues before they appeared and before family members had developed rigid and opposing opinions.

By anticipating problems, he forestalled some of the anguish that we see in famous families that destroy themselves through family feuds. If you're in the mood for some sobering cautionary tales, visit FORBES, http://www.forbes.com/2011/07/13/family-fortune-fights_slide.html.

HOW TO MAKE YOUR FAMILY BUSINESS LAST

If you visit that site, you'll read the stories of anguish, misery and destruction, that come about when families don't get the human relations part of the equation right. Frank was aware that only 3% of family businesses make it past the third generation and he wanted to beat those odds. After all, he was a family man to the core and handing on his legacy of producing a needed product and providing tens of thousands of jobs was all-important to him.

By temperament, Frank had no interest in reinventing the wheel, and if there were professionals who had expertise in these matters, it was predictable that he would seek them out. He chose John Ward in 1994 and the relationship with the Family Business Consulting Business continues to this day, although John Ward has now retired and Frank has gone to his great reward.

Today Jennifer Pendergast continues a relationship initiated 23 years ago.

Since John Ward was the family business advisor Frank chose, I'm concluding, with Ward's permission, a list you might find helpful. It's from his book, "How to Choose and Use Advisors."

Checklist for Choosing Advisors

>Do they have experience working with family businesses?

>Are they abreast of literature on serving the family business?

>Do they subscribe to respected publications in the field?

Are they respected by other family business professionals?

Have they written or spoken publicly on serving family businesses?

Can they provide references from successful family businesses?

Do they network among other family business advisors?

Do they attend family business conferences?

Are they familiar with the dynamics of families-known among professionals as "family systems theory"?

Do they show interest and concern for family factors as they affect your business?

Resources:

You can reach Drew Mendoza, the managing principal of the firm John Ward co-founded, at the Family Business Consulting Group by e-mailing him at: Mendoza@theFBCG.com

How to Choose and Use Advisors: Getting the Best Professional Family Business Advice (A Family Business Publication) December 2010 by C. Aronoff and J. Ward

SECTION II

PROBLEMS? DON'T LET THEM TURN INTO THREE-GENERATION TRAGEDIES

INTRODUCTION

A high-functioning family can be one of the greatest sources of joy in your life. But alas, when things are going badly, the pain of a conflict can permeate every hour and every day. A conflict gone wrong can add sadness to the lives of the next three generations.

This section is first-aid for some of the problems you may encounter. I wrote it with the hope that you can find tools to keep conflicts from ballooning into tragedies.

The biggest message you'll read here is, when you're in a conflict, explore every avenue you can before going to litigation.

The reason I say this is, I've talked with dozens of family business advisors, and every one of them has mentioned that when you get to the point of actually litigating, that's almost a sure sign that the family is over. I've watched in families where they've ended up in court, and in the process, torpedoed the family legacy, and caused strife that's still talked about three generations later.

Something that's on my mind as I write this: I recently met an 80-year old man at a family business conference, and this man had endured a family lawsuit a few years ago that split his family. His children no longer speak to him, and everything he had worked for plus the legacy that would normally have given his life meaning, has been shattered. He was thinking of suicide.

It's from the experience of talking with people like this gentleman that I feel so strongly about trying to solve problems before they reach the point of no return. I hope the tools you'll read about in this section can help you.

Actually, what I really hope is that you don't need them and never will. But they're here in case you do.

CHAPTER 17

A LEGAL DISPUTE? FIX IT FASTER, CHEAPER, AND WITH LESS AGONY!

Are you enduring a fight related to your family business? One where you and a fellow family member might end up in court?

If so, dear friends, what you're about to read could be the most valuable thing you come across in the *How to Make Your Family Business Last.* I'm putting this topic first in this section for just this reason.

What you're about to read is a way out of a serious, potentially family-wrecking dilemma. It's a way of fixing disputes that's faster, cheaper, more humane, and that doesn't have to leave lasting scars. It can exponentially increase the chances of your family staying intact across the generations.

In the experience of everyone I know, by the time an individual is willing to take a dispute to court, the chances of putting things back together approach zero. Lawsuits can be so painful, so expensive, and so destructive that I know of families that still talk about them three generations later.

Fortunately, this never happened in the families I'm closest to. Both the Hendersons and the Perdues abide by "family covenant" in which it's ok to fight and get issues out on the table, but it's never ok to go to either the press or lawyers with a dispute. I think we absorbed "We do not wash our dirty linen in public" as thoroughly as we absorbed, "Thou shalt not kill."

Now all this may sound good in theory, but in practice, we are all human beings and legitimate disputes do arise. Is there a way of dealing with them short of going to court?

Yes.

Collaborative Law

According to Professor David Hoffman from the Harvard Law School, Collaborative Law is a relatively new branch of law that deals with dispute resolution. According to Hoffman, the Collaborative Law approach means that disputes can get resolved in a manner that both sides perceive as fairer.

But just what is Collaborative law? And how does it differ from other approaches to dispute resolution?

In Collaborative law, a major feature is lawyers as well as the mental health and financial professionals who are part of the process, agree ahead of time that their purpose in being there is to achieve a settlement. There are teeth in this approach because if the dispute ends in litigation instead of settlement, the lawyers are fired. They are not allowed to represent either party in litigation.

Huge benefits accrue from this approach. With litigation off the table, the incentives change from, "We're fighting to win!" to, "We're cooperating to achieve a win-win."

A win-win in this case means that settlement is achieved while keeping time, money, nerves, and emotional pain in check.

HOW TO MAKE YOUR FAMILY BUSINESS LAST

Dealing with emotional pain represents one of the biggest differences between the Collaborative process and a litigated approach. The Collaborative process specifically addresses emotional issues, whether in a family business dispute, a divorce, a prenuptial meeting or any other area where people feel a need for the legal system. The Collaborative team brings emotional issues to the forefront and uses mental health professionals as part of a team approach to finding solutions.

We've all heard stories of divorcing couples spending tens of thousands of dollars in legal fees to argue about pets or one piece of furniture. Hoffman and his colleagues recognize that in most such cases, the couples are not arguing about dogs, cats or furniture. Instead, they are reacting to the psychological pain they are experiencing.

Hoffman has also seen that another issue, cognitive bias, keeps people from arriving at a settlement in absence of the Collaborative approach. One of the biases is our own memories of an event may be firm and vivid--yet wrong.

Hoffman likes to tell the story of a man who remembered the time he and his wife were walking down Fifth Avenue in New York. The man's wife happened to glance over to her left, and to her astonishment, there was Jackie Onassis looking at her and enthusiastically waving.

The man's wife doesn't know Jackie, but Jackie keeps waving. The wife isn't quite sure what's going on, but she looks behind her to see if Jackie is waving at somebody else.

But there's nobody there. And Jackie is still waving at

her! The wife tentatively waves back, and Jackie responds by waving still harder!

Just then a cab screeches to a halt, and Jackie jumps in. Mrs. Onassis had been waving to hail a cab.

It's a fun story, no?

But is it accurate?

The man's wife agreed with every part of the story except one important point: the wife is certain her husband wasn't there. She had told him the entire story when she returned home that night.

Interestingly, the husband is just as certain that he was there. "I remember it so clearly," he insisted, adding, "I can still remember what I was wearing and I remember how the sun felt on my skin!"

Of course, only one of those stories can be true. It illustrates that we frequently weave our own inaccurate stories when remembering events.

When Professor Hoffman was telling this story, it was to the New York Association of Collaborative Professionals (NYACP), a group of lawyers, finance experts, and mental health professionals who practice Collaborative Law in the NYC Metro region. He himself got the story from an NPR broadcast hosted by Ira Glass.

These Collaborative professionals nodded in agreement over the essential truth of the story Hoffman had just told: that there's much more to getting to settlement than "Just the facts, Ma'am." People's experiences of reality frequently don't match, and to achieve settlement, the emotions, feelings and cognitive biases need to be understood and included in the resolution process.

The goal of the practitioners of Collaborative law is to provide you and the counterparty in you dispute with a safe and dignified environment that reduces conflict and minimizes its impact on your family, your business and your life. They work to resolve your legal disputes with *you* making the decision as opposed to judges, magistrates or court personnel.

Would both sides of the dispute you're enduring be willing to try a Collaborative approach to resolving the dispute? They're prime candidates if they go along with most of the following propositions.

Checklist for the Collaborative Solution Approach

You're a candidate for a Collaborative solution if you agree that:

> Arguments are seldom about what they're about.

> Mental health professionals can help resolve underlying conflicts, often ones that stem from unresolved tensions from childhood.

> Hiring advocates whose incentives are linked to resolution may mean a speedier resolution.

> A quicker resolution means lower legal costs.

> Hiring advocates who are looking out for the good of both parties decreases the danger of an irreparable rupture in the family.

Resolution is essential because it's not just the disputant who are hurt by an argument in a business family; it's all the other stakeholders including employees, stockholders, bankers, the community, and even future generations.

Once litigation starts, it can cause people to harden their positions and become irrational, wanting to win at all costs.

In addition, the incentive for lawyers at this point is to focus on their client. This perspective may not benefit the family as a whole.

Your family is so important that it's a danger to your long-term happiness to have it threatened by litigation.

I wish I could materialize out of this page and plead with anyone in your family who is considering litigation to consider the alternative of collaborative law. This really matters.

The pain and heartache and regret that I've watched when people take the route of litigation is endless. They imagine that they can outsource litigation to their lawyers and a short while later, take home their winnings from the lawsuit.

Instead, the lawsuit is likely to result in unimaginable stress coupled with a bottomless sinkhole of wasted time and nerve-jarring cost. A lawsuit can also mean a permanent rupture in the bonds that keep a family together.

Because of the stakes, which as far as your family goes, couldn't be higher, please, please consider Collaborative law.

Resources:

If you'd like more information on Collaborative approaches, visit the International Academy of Collaborative Professionals at https://www.collaborativepractice.com.

David A. Hoffman, Esq. can be reached at: 617-439-4700, ext. 201, DHoffman@blc.law, or visit the Boston Law Collaborative at https://blc.law .

Two other practitioners are: Charles McEvily, Cmcevily@aol.com, and Roxane Polak, RoxanePolak@gmail.com.

Mediation: Another Alternative to Litigation

Drew Mendoza, Managing Principal of the Family Business Consulting Group observed, "In my 23 years of experience with 2,400 clients, I've never seen even one family business that started down the road of litigation be able successfully to pull back."

Since there's so much to lose when family members are considering litigation, are there other approaches to consider, in addition to the Collaborative Law approach described in the last chapter?

Mediation is another such approach. I can't know which would fit your family's needs best, but since there's so much at stake, why not take a look at both approaches?

HOW TO MAKE YOUR FAMILY BUSINESS LAST

According to the Harvard Law School's David Hoffman, one of the major advantages of mediation is, it can sidestep a major danger for a family business when members are represented by their own lawyers
When family members hire their own lawyers, these lawyers may feel they serve their clients best through adversarial advocacy. The problem with this, according to Hoffman, is, "Adversarial lawyers usually evoke an adversarial response, and this can escalate the conflict."

Selecting a mediator gives a family business a far better chance at de-escalation. At its best, mediation can help both sides understand each other better and it's very best, mediation can help the participants grow as a family.

Bernard Kliska, Ph.D. has worked with Drew Mendoza at the Family Business Consulting Group, and he has strong views on the value of a mediator: "A mediated settlement has a better chance of soothing not just the business problem but also the troubled relationships that exacerbated it."

He goes on to say, "The greatest value that a mediator can offer is not to decide a winner or loser but to help facilitate a pertinent discussion between the parties. When a mediation is used effectively even the most difficult issues can be resolved to the satisfaction of the parties, without the time, expense and emotional toll exacted by other means of dispute resolution.
The mediator can help the parties communicate and develop a mutually acceptable solution. In Kliska's view, this kind of resolution has a good chance of being carried out because, having helped craft it, both sides own it and have a vested interest in making it work.

Given that mediation has so much going for it, how do you select a mediator?

Checklist for Selecting a Mediator

David Hoffman recommends considering three characteristics when choosing a mediator:

- o **Competence.** Does the candidate have experience with family business conflicts, and if so, how much experience? Are there lawyers or mediation participants who can vouch for the mediator's skill in the family business arena?

- o **Chemistry**. Hiring a mediator for a family business dispute is a bit like hiring a therapist or business adviser. Qualifications are usually not the deciding factor if the interpersonal connection does not feel right.

- o **Tenacity.** In interviewing potential mediators, one can ask about their experience in their most difficult cases.

Hoffman also recommends the following processes for choosing a lawyer of a lawyer will be involved in mediation:

Interview the Candidate.
Have the family members interview all the candidates who are interested in serving as counsel to any of the parties. Then the family members decide together which lawyers to hire and whom they will represent. By interviewing and hiring lawyers in this unconventional way, family members can feel more confident that the

tenor of the negotiations will not sink to the lowest common denominator of adversarial activity, and that all the lawyers support the family's goal of an amicable settlement.

If lawyers must be involved, try getting referrals from mediators.
Mediators can be a good resource for lawyer referrals. They have seen numerous lawyers in action and can recommend those who have good track records for resolving conflicts constructively.

If some members have representation, all members should have the advice they need to participate.
In some cases, one family member may feel that he/she wants to have his/her lawyer present, while other family members prefer not to have their lawyers present. This difference may be related to cost considerations or concern about levelling the playing field if one party feels less skillful as a negotiator. While there is no rule in mediation requiring all parties to have lawyers with them, if some do, all participants in the mediation should feel that they have the advice and support that they need to participate.

The stakes involved in a family business dispute are so enormous that it's worth going the extra mile to avoid litigation that could rip the family apart for generations. If you're approaching the precipice of a public family dispute and litigation, there's still time to pull back. Using either a mediator or a practitioner of Collaborative Law.

Resources:

Drew Mendoza and Bernard Kliska can be reached at the Family Business Consulting Group, 773-604-5005 or visit the website at: https://www.thefbcg.com. Mendoza's email is: Mendoza@theFBCG.com, and Kliska's is bkkliska@aol.com .

David A. Hoffman, Esq. can be reached at: 617-439-4700, ext. 201, DHoffman@blc.law, or visit the Boston Law Collaborative at https://blc.law .

CHAPTER 18

PROS AND CONS OF STAYING IN A FAMILY BUSINESS

There's one additional subject to address before we leave the subject of problems that may confront a business family. What if the issue you're dealing with is whether to sell the company or not?

Do your family members struggle with whether to stay a family-owned business? I recommend getting the issues out in the open and dealing with them.

But meanwhile, I'd love to share my experiences with you. I've been part of a family business that was sold, and I'm also part of one that continues to this day.

Although there are some advantages to selling, in my experience, being part of a continuing family business is, oh, about 10,000 times better than selling.

Here's what happened. The Sheraton Hotels were a family-owned company and my father and then my brother ran it. On my father's death, the family sold the company. The Perdue family, in contrast, is now a fourth-generation company and the fifth generation is coming on strong.

What Are the Pros and Cons of Each Approach?

In the case of Sheraton, the pros of selling the company included more cash than any of my family members had ever seen. It meant the ability to found other companies, which my two brothers and I did.

HOW TO MAKE YOUR FAMILY BUSINESS LAST

For my two sisters, it meant philanthropy and public service on a scale that wouldn't have been possible otherwise. For all five of us, the money that came our way was a blessing beyond imagination because of the new businesses and the philanthropy that it made possible.

Further, we've been able to stay together as a family, almost as close as if we still owned the hotel chain. We sold Sheraton in the late 1960s, but we've remained totally intact and possibly closer than ever, given that there's no reason ever to disagree about family business issues.

The family foundation and its activities keep us together, as do the family reunions that started in 1890. On top of that, our history and our traditions have kept us together even without a jointly-owned family business.

The downside was, I don't think a publicly held company would ever care as much about the Sheraton employees as the family did. And in the early years immediately following the sale, the new management didn't seem to have the high standards for the hotels that we did when we owned the company.

For roughly ten years, I wouldn't even patronize a Sheraton Hotel. My reason was that when I'd see a stained carpet or cracked glass on a display case, I'd sense that the standards that made "Sheraton, the Proudest Name in Hotels," were no longer enforced.

It was too depressing. Actually, it made me miserable and I made a point of not setting foot in a Sheraton hotel for at least a decade.

By the way, I don't feel that way now. I can feel proud when I visit a Sheraton today because obviously the current owners, Marriott Hotels, have impressively high standards. I like Marriott enough so that I even joined the Marriott rewards system.

Something bigger than being concerned about the new owners is something that's hard to describe. The sale was traumatic for family members. Unless you've been through it, you might not guess how much of your identity can be tied up in being part of a family-owned business.

Of course, it can't be even remotely as terrible as, for example, being a refugee. But even so, on a drastically smaller scale, there can be a sense of being uprooted and that your world has been damaged and irretrievably changed. There was a surprisingly large emotional price to pay for the financial benefits that came from selling the company.

Reasons for Keeping the Family Business in the Family: I see only Pros

The Perdue family took a different path and I'm happy as can be that the family business is still in the family. There are a host of reasons:

Identity. Frank used to say that many people spend their entire lives looking for meaning, hungering to be part of something bigger than themselves. In his view, "A family business is a built-in, ready-made answer to that." When the family business stays in the family, members don't need to endure the sense of rootlessness and loss of meaning that I went through when the Henderson family sold Sheraton.

Control. Family businesses have much greater control than a publicly-owned company. When we wanted to get into organic chicken, despite enormous barriers to entry, we could think a decade ahead, and we could deal with doing less well competitively as we learned how to do it and then created the infrastructure to support it. We didn't have to accommodate public stockholders who were counting on competitive results each quarter.

Trust. I love it that I know the family members are looking out for each other and have a loyalty to something higher than themselves.

Long Term Values. While public companies are up against quarterly reports and the demand for short-term profitability, family businesses have the luxury of putting long-term values over short-term gains. We can embrace strategies that put customers and employees first and emphasize social responsibility.

My favorite example of long term values, in the case of Perdue, is, we undertook to revamp our headquarters in an environmentally sound way. We did it so well that our renovated headquarters building was one of the few in all of Maryland to receive a LEED Platinum designation.

LEED stands for Leadership in Energy and Environmental Design. During the years we were working on this, there was a spike in grain prices and it was lean years for the chicken industry. We could have abandoned the sustainability efforts, but instead chose to see it through because the family and the company put a high value on sustainability.

You and your family members will have your own reasons to decide whether to keep the family business in the family. And, possibly it isn't even a choice when outside factors are determining what you need to do.

But if it is a choice, consider the non-financial aspects of the decision. If you decide to sell, it's likely to be forever.

Checklist of Considerations for Keeping the Family Business in the Family

How important are the following?

Keeping the Family Business in the Family

Family pride and identity

Maintaining the culture that made the company succeed

Looking out for the people who work there

Control, being able to make long term decisions as opposed to worrying about the next quarterly report to the stockholders

Trust, at its best family members look out for each other

Long term values

Reasons for Cashing Out

Being able to have resources for philanthropy

Having cash available for new entrepreneurial ventures

Life is simpler when you don't have to take relatives into account

You don't have confidence in the current leadership

CHAPTER 19

Gold Diggers: Forewarned is Forearmed

When I was growing up in the 1950s, I swooned over the 1956 Bing Crosby song, *True Love.*

While I give to you and you give to me
True love, true love
So, on and on it will always be
True love, true love –forever more!

This song shaped how I believed love really was.

For me, it was disillusioning beyond imagination when at the beginning of my freshman year at Radcliffe, I spent an evening in our dormitory's lounge, listening to seven classmates talk. They were systematically paging through the catalogue of our Harvard freshmen classmates.

My classmates were assessing what the Harvard men we'd be meeting were likely to inherit.

"His father is giving him a million dollars for his 21st birthday," said one blond, long-legged beauty, referring to one of the men in the catalogue

"His family is in steel," said another, pointing to a dark-haired guy in the catalogue.

"Oh look, this one---his family owns the world's largest scientific glass instruments company," said a woman from Boston, checking out a seriously attractive blond guy.

HOW TO MAKE YOUR FAMILY BUSINESS LAST

"Ooh, I can't believe this guy is one of our classmates! He's a member of the Cuban rum family," enthused a woman from Florida.

These young women were busily sharing their plans for meeting and attracting their wealthy Harvard classmates and imagining being married to them. They all agreed that it was as easy to fall in love with a rich man as with a poor man.

Up to that moment it had never occurred to me to think of love in anything but the purely romantic way that dear Bing Crosby taught in his "True Love" song.

Don't Make the Mistake My Parents Made

Please don't make the mistake that I feel my parents made of keeping their children ignorant of the fact that they will encounter people with dubious motives. Such people exist and you can't defend against them if you don't recognize this.

By the way, I have no problem with someone who is attracted to earned wealth (as opposed to inherited wealth). An individual with enough force of personality, insight, intelligence and energy to achieve financial success may have a lot going for him or her. People may be rightfully attracted to such a person.

My issue is gold diggers who target people not for their personality, but for their wealth. A true gold-digger exploits his or her target the way a parasite exploits a host.

HOW TO MAKE YOUR FAMILY BUSINESS LAST

Some Are Obvious, Most Are Not

If I were warning people about gold diggers, I'd start out by saying that some of the gold diggers they'll come across may be simply astoundingly obvious. A man I once dated briefly (he was a Nobel prize winner) simply asked what I was worth. (I know lots of people may have wondered, but Mr. Nobel Prize Winner *actually asked.)*

And then, to top it off, he made a guess that was so close to the truth that I had to wonder if he had done some sophisticated research on me. This was not subtle.

However, a person's interest in your finances is not usually so flagrantly obvious. In the case of fortune-hunters, the best of the breed can be amazingly convincing. As my late father used to say, "If a con man looked like a con man, he wouldn't be a con man."

There is a breed of vulture who knows how to be the friend or lover you have always dreamed of but never could find. Unfortunately, this isn't a hard role for a psychopath to play because they are always, always on their guard, they feel no discomfort in dishonesty, they can lie and take advantage without working up a sweat. These kinds of vultures are driven by a single goal... themselves.

When someone love bombs you, agrees with everything you say, seems to share all your dreams and aspirations, and maybe on top of that is sexy beyond your wildest fantasies, it may be a sign that you've at last met the right person.

Or equally, it could mean that you're dealing with a con-person, someone who wants your money, your lifestyle, your prestige, your contacts, and maybe your scalp.

Ah, but how do you discover which is which? And along the way, how do you strike the delicate balance between being too suspicious and too trusting?

Checklist for Avoiding Fortune Hunters

> **Listen to your "Spidey sense."**
> This refers to Spider-Man's ability to sense danger. When you're feeling that something isn't right, it may be because your subconscious picked up things that your conscious mind missed–or didn't want to see. Pay attention. If you feel it strongly, don't let yourself get talked out of it too easily. It could save you a life of misery. In most of the cases that I know of that ended badly, the individuals did have nagging suspicions but talked themselves out of it—to their unending financial and emotional regret.
>
> **Is the person trying to rush you into something?**
> It can be entirely legitimate, but it can also be that they don't want you to have time to think. As a personal insurance policy, don't allow yourself to be rushed; the longer you know a person, the harder it is for them to hide their true character.
>
> **Look at how they act in daily life.**
> Life coach Martha Beck likes to say, "How you do something is how you do everything." I couldn't agree more. The thing I tend to notice most of all—it's like an X-Ray into a person's

character—is how they treat waiters or cab drivers or people behind the counter in a store. Are they inconsiderate? Rude? Belittling? A person with integrity tends to treat all people with respect, and if your romantic interest treats people he doesn't care about like dirt, it's possible that how he's acting with you is a mask for his real self, a mask that will come off later in the relationship, after he's gotten what he wants from you.

Are they in debt?
This is a very serious red flag. There are people who want free money and the possibility exists that they've targeted you as the magic answer to their financial situation.

Do they pay their bills on time?
If not, and if this behavior is habitual, it's a first cousin to stealing. The person is ignoring a reciprocal obligation that honest people take seriously. Would you trust someone who's dishonest with others to be above-board with you?

Do they need you to finance their life?
For example, do they need money from you to help tide them over until the money they're expecting comes in? I have never seen this kind of situation work out well. I've seen dozens of cases where a woman deeply in love, wanting to help the man she loves, and "understanding" how he got in the predicament, will do anything to help him out so that they'll have a lifetime together. There may be cases where this doesn't lead to heartbreak, but based on every case I

know of, I wouldn't bet on it. The creepy thing is, a confidence man or woman can be exceptionally convincing; you just *know* that he or she is telling you the truth and the problem is temporary and completely not his or her fault. Oh, and you have the feeling of utter certainty that you completely understand the situation and you'd almost be willing to stake your life on the certainty that this case is different. Unfortunately, it's probably not.

How often do they make excuses?
In the scales of trustworthiness, an action weighs an elephant. An excuse weighs a mouse. Two excuses weigh a cockroach. Three excuses weigh a bacteria. Four excuses, on the scale of trustworthiness, weigh about what a virus weighs, and a virus typically weighs $1/100^{th}$ of what a bacteria weighs. In other words, if there are many excuses, they're apt to count for virtually nothing. In the cases that I know of, the person who habitually makes excuses ("The bank wire didn't go through!" "My secretary screwed up!" "My briefcase was stolen and it had the money in it!") has given you reasons to wonder about everything else they say. Jung's saying, "You are what you do, not what you say," is a good guide.

Notice the person's relationship with others.
Does the person have a caring family? Long-standing professional relationships? Long-term friends? If you want to avoid fortune-hunters, get to know an individual's family and make sure you've met and spent time with people who've known the person for years.

Conceit and boastfulness should ring alarm bells.

When someone tells you how trustworthy he or she is, right there that's a red alert. Just as Einstein wouldn't have sat down and told you how smart he was, and Bill Gates doesn't have to tell you how rich he is, a trustworthy person doesn't have to tell you how trustworthy he is.

Flattery is another red flag.

It's bonding and it makes you feel good, and it can be a genuine expression of his or her feelings. Besides, who doesn't want to hear, "You're the soul-mate I've been waiting for all my life!" or "You're the only one who's ever truly understood me!" But weighing against the possibility that these words are wrenched from the depths of the person's heart, is the somber fact that flattery can also be an incredibly manipulative tool in the hands of someone who wants what you have.

Keep in mind that words are cheap.

Words may convey the deepest, most soul-felt feelings. Ah, but then again, they may not. A guy once told me that he could "score" five nights a week on one of the Internet dating sites. How did he do it? "I just tell the woman I want to sleep with, 'I love you.' There are no three words in the English language that get you greater results for less effort."

Lying is a deal-breaker.

I agree with the old Chinese saying that lying is acceptable under only two circumstances: to save a life or to flatter a woman. Trust is all-important and if the person is a liar on one thing, you've already seen that he or she has a fragile relationship with the truth. When a person has shown that they're capable of lying, you may be right to doubt everything else they say,

They violate social norms with no guilt.
A simple example I can think of is a guy who would always line-jump to be at the front of the security line at airports. He didn't want to be treated like cattle and therefore felt no need to follow the rules of waiting his turn along with everyone else. It turned out that this was a sample of how he acted in all his dealings. The rules didn't apply to *him*. Beware the person who violates social norms in small things, like line-jumping, because they may violate social norms in bigger things as well.

People have an extraordinary propensity to describe themselves when they're describing others.
This isn't always true, but if the new person in your life makes a practice of describing others as dishonest, double-dealing, irresponsible, malicious, violent, litigious, or even murderous, you know it's on their minds and you're entitled to wonder if he or she is describing himself or herself. My instinct at this point, assuming the behavior isn't a rare occurrence, would be to run away, far and fast.

When did the relationship start?
If Mr. or Ms. Perfect shows up soon after the death of your wealthy spouse, or parent, this is a time for extreme red-alert caution. There are

wonderful people out there and maybe you found one, but I remember when my husband passed away, my cousin Ned Horn warned, "Fifty people are reading your husband's obituary right now, and they're calculating what they need to do to meet you." The number Ned gave was an underestimate, but in principle, he was right. In short order, scores of dicey people began showing up, each offering "to help" in one way or another. It wasn't hard to spot their intentions.

If you're an extra-nice person, be extra on-guard against these kinds of predators. Every instinct you have makes you want to believe the good in people. The problem is you may fit what Cicero said more than 2000 years ago: "It is as hard for the good person to suspect evil, as it is for the evil person to suspect good." Our minds tend to project onto others our own view of the world, and your projection of goodness and fair play onto the other person may be right…but it also could be disastrously wrong. Because of your kind nature, you may have unusual difficulty processing the fact that a predator isn't as kind and honest as you are.

Resources:

Ah dear friends, I normally have books and websites for advice at the end of my checklists, but in this case, finding resources other than what I've observed in my life has been difficult. You can find a plethora of books and websites telling you how to *be* a successful fortune hunter. I, however, am in the business of helping you thwart them.

In general, I haven't found many resources that specifically advise you about how to avoid fortune hungers.

Two shining exceptions are the website www.LoveFraud.com and the book, *Red Flags of Love Fraud: 10 Signs You're Dating a Sociopath.* Donna Andersen, who is responsible for the website and the book, has made a life study of the distressing phenomenon of people who fake love in order to get money, status, connections or whatever else you have that they want. The hallmarks of her writing are compassion, empathy, and realism.

Since you and your family are members of a family business, you may be vulnerable to the Ned Horn Hypothesis, that many people will have ulterior motives for wanting to get involved with you. Donna Andersen's work can help you recognize them and avoid them.

CHAPTER 20

Prenups: Necessary--But, You Can Make Them Less Stressful[1]

You can find issues more uncomfortable than prenuptial agreements.

But not many.

If you want to prevent problems in the family business, it's important to address the issue of prenuptial agreements. Even better, develop a family policy on it.

One of the reasons prenups are such a delicate subject is that people view them from amazingly different points of view. One of my granddaughter's professors told her that asking anyone for a prenup was so demeaning and exploitive and showed such a lack of trust that even asking for one would be grounds for breaking an engagement.

On the other side, a social friend of mine has the attitude, "Anyone who won't sign a prenup, is after your money." She told her son that if a woman were unwilling to sign a prenup, that would be disqualifying. "Why should she be paid for marrying you?" the mother asked. She also felt that a prenup was the perfect way of finding out whether the other side's motives were financial or not.

---

[1] Copyright Family Firm Institute.
https://ffipractitioner.org/2017/01/04/prenuptial-agreements-uncomfortable-and-necessary/

My own view is somewhere in the middle, but I do believe that for members of a family business, marriage isn't about just two individuals. A divorce could impact the family, the employees, the lenders, the customers, and the community.

Businesses Can Be Destroyed When There's a Divorce and No Prenup

Like me, you probably know or have read about divorces that damaged or destroyed an on-going business. The collateral damage from a bankruptcy or hostile takeover or brand damage can be disastrous for countless innocent bye-standers. A prenup is an insurance policy taken out on behalf of this larger constituency.

Assuming you've come down on the side of having a prenup, (and I hope you have), how do you deal with the fact that marriage is more than an intimate partnership, it's also a financial partnership? How do you make something so inherently fraught less painful?

The good news is, the relatively new legal field of Collaborative law can help. As mentioned in an earlier chapter, a Collaborative approach always involves not just lawyers representing each side, but also a mental health professional, and often a neutral financial expert. Instead of being adversarial, the Collaborative team's focus is on getting to an agreement where both sides feel good about it.

To get to the "feel good" part of the agreement, the team consciously addresses underlying emotional issues. Roxane Polak, Ph.D., a licensed mental health professional who frequently participates in Collaborative prenuptial agreements, likes to point out that, "Arguments about money are never really about the money."

Money Quarrels: They're Not about What They're About

An example Dr. Polak gives is, "Suppose you're a woman whose childhood included weekend visitations with your divorced father. At these times, your father lavished you with expensive gifts. Over time you may have learned to equate valuable gifts with love. But now," Polak continues, "let's say you're paired up with a guy whose parents remembered the depression, and they instilled in him a permanent sense of financial insecurity. They brought him up with the attitude, 'You've got to save for the future! You could lose everything!'"

Initially, this couple is going to have a problem with their prenup. The woman may feel that the guy is some combination of cheap and unloving. The guy, on the other hand, is starting to feel that his beloved is greedy, materialistic, and hasn't a care for the future.

The underlying problem is that they are likely to have no understanding of where the other person is coming from. As Dr. Polak says, "Most people come from families that never talked about money. They may not even have the tools to talk about money."

Fortunately, with the help of mental health professionals who are part of the Collaborative team, the two can learn to understand each other. Typically, as the understanding grows, so does sympathy for the other's position.

"When people have a greater understanding of what money means to each of the parties," Polak continues, "they have a better chance of reaching an agreement that seems fair and that addresses what matters to each of them."

Collaborative professionals know that there are a whole host of problems hiding under the rubric of money. Money might represent such things as: a means of control; a tool for expressing rebelliousness against a parent; protection against insecurity; status and social position; integrity involving promises made to prior children; or a litmus test about a person's real motives for the relationship.

For Polak, there are enormous advantages to understanding what money symbolizes. When the whole collaborative team gets involved, they work on getting to solutions that aren't zero-sum, but rather ones that involve understanding and sympathy for each other and that both parties can endorse.

The process often involves discovering that the parties have different interests stemming from their different backgrounds. The archetype of this is the story from Fisher and Ury's classic book, *Getting to Yes.* Collaborative law professor David Hoffman from Harvard likes to quote the story when describing the benefits of Collaborative law. "Two kids were arguing over an orange, and the parent solved it by slicing the orange in half. But a better approach would have been asking not about the orange, but what each child's interest in the orange was. It turns out that one child wanted to make juice and the other wanted the rind for baking."

For Hoffman, "The Collaborative approach works to find who wants juice and who wants rind, so both parties can be pleased with the resolution."

Get the True Interests Out on the Table

Getting the true interests on the table is likely to result in a more amicable agreement. But there's more to it than even that. "The process of writing a prenup," Dr. Polak says, "probably won't feel good, but it's excellent for discovering how well you and your intended handle important disagreements. A prenup isn't the last disagreement you'll have, and the prenup is a kind of X-ray into how well you'll do in handling future disagreements."

A problem with any prenup is, how do you go about bringing up this fiendishly ticklish subject? Presumably you're in love, and here you are telling your intended that you aren't sure the marriage will last.

According to Charles McEvily, Esq. you've got two choices. You can work it through, or pretend it isn't there and live with the consequences. Like Polak and Hoffman, McEvily feels that the strongest beginning to a marriage is to face the tough questions.

The conversation, whether over a candle lit dinner, in bed, or at the kitchen table, could begin with a discussion about marriage being a financial partnership as well as an intimate one. "This conversation is going to raise fears," admits McEvily. "It's going to make the couple recheck what this relationship is about. But still, they need to plunge in and have the conversation."

McEvily recommends bringing up the subject of a

prenuptial agreement a minimum of three months before the wedding. Six months would be better, and best is when the couple is first seriously discussing marriage. It's easier when there aren't looming deadlines plus it takes time to assemble a Collaborative law team. Further, waiting until the last minute may have a "take it or leave it" feel to it. In most cases, the party who's presented with a last minute prenup will take it, given the embarrassment of canceling the wedding the last minute.

An additional problem, according to Hoffman, is that a last minute prenup may not be legally enforceable. "If the prenup is ever challenged, a spouse could claim that *not* signing didn't feel like an option because the wedding invitations had already been sent."

Even beyond the enforceability issue, McEvily has seen that, "There's a cost to starting out the marriage this way. Over time it's apt to grate and turn into a major impediment to a healthy marriage." In his experience in as many as 10% of the cases where this happens, it means the end of the marriage.

Prenups are a scary and difficult topic. They're not just about money; they're about deeply felt emotions. And in the case of a family business, they're about all the other stakeholders who could be harmed by a difficult divorce. Fortunately, the recent practice of Collaborative law can make it less scary and less difficult.

Checklist for Prenuptial Agreements

> **Have a general family policy on prenuptial agreements that applies to everyone.** Make sure all family members know the policy. With a

blanket policy, a soon-to-be new family member will not feel that it's directed at him or her.

Emphasize the idea of the couple as part of a larger entity.
Talk with family members or include it in newsletters that in a family business, marriage isn't about just two people and it's about all the many people who have a stake in the family business such as employees and customers.

The prenup discussion is a preparation on how to work through difficult issues. Let marriageable aged family members know that how the couple handles this difficult discussion is excellent practice for some of the many difficult conversations they'll have in the future.

Have the discussion about prenups as soon as it's serious. Encourage marriageable age family members to bring up the family policy on pre-nups as soon as the relationship looks as if it's heading towards marriage.

Do not wait until the last minute. Make sure everyone knows that waiting until the last minute can start the marriage off on the wrong foot and may result in an agreement that's legally unenforceable.

Resources:

If you'd like more information on Collaborative approaches you can start by going to: Abby Rosmarin, Esq., LMHC, the Executive Director of the NYACP at arosmarin@nycollaborativeprofessionals.org or visit http://www.nycollaborativeprofessionals.org. In addition, you can contact collaborative professionals worldwide by visiting the International Academy of Collaborative Professionals at https://www.collaborativepractice.com.

To contact individuals mentioned in this chapter:

David A. Hoffman, Esq., DHoffman@blc.law.

Charles McEvily, Esq., www.McEvily-Law.com; Cmcevily@aol.com area.

Roxane Polak, Ph.D. RoxanePolak@gmail.com

CHAPTER 21

Substance Abuse: There's a Lot You Can Do to Help Prevent It

The consequences of addiction...well, I don't have to tell you because I bet you know about these consequences all too well.

Think for a moment of a case you know of. Did it involve a promising child who dropped out of college? Broken-hearted parents? An overdose?

We all know that substance abuse can be a catastrophe, especially when it's a family business that's affected. What can you do to give the young people in your life the best chance of avoiding it?

We're Aiming at a Culture of, "Our family Doesn't do drugs."

I love the example of my step grandson-in-law, Keith Eliason. His two sons are about to become Eagle Scouts, and since the youngsters are clearly turning out so well, I asked him how he handled the possibility of drugs. His answer?

"I've beat it into them from the start that drugs are not what an intelligent person does. Doing drugs is a choice that someone who doesn't like himself makes. I've always encouraged them to think things through and make intelligent choices and obviously doing drugs is not an intelligent choice in life."

He's not wishy-washy about it. He has no problem taking a stand. It's an approach (one that I admire mightily) from a wise and loving father who's also an amateur. What does a professional say?

Joe Califano was a Cabinet Member under President Johnson, and he has devoted his life to dealing with substance abuse. As founder of the National Center on Addiction and Substance Abuse, he knows factors that make young people less vulnerable to drugs and alcohol. There are things that you all can do.

Checklist for Avoiding Substance Abuse

Be a good example.
Don't abuse illegal drugs or alcohol.

Keep dangerous prescription drugs out of their reach.
Almost half of kids abusing addictive prescription drugs got them from the family medicine cabinet.

Frame substance abuse as a moral issue.
Let the young people in your life know that you consider substance abuse to be morally wrong. Children are far more influenced by parents who consider substance abuse to be morally wrong (and stupid) than they are influenced by whether the substance is illegal or not. As Califano says, "Parent Power is the most effective way to discourage teen drug use. Most kids get their sense of morality from their parents. Parents, you cannot outsource your role to law enforcement."

Demand that your children's schools be drug free. 1 in 5 middle schoolers and almost 2/3 of high schoolers attend schools where drugs are used, kept and sold. Your child is at far greater risk at one of these schools.

Attend religious services. Whether Catholic, Protestant, Jewish, or Muslim, children who attend services are three times less likely to smoke and drink.

Have dinner together. Young people who have dinner with their parents at least 5 times a week are far less likely to smoke, drink or use drugs than kids who have family dinners less than 3 times a week.

So, to improve your odds of having drug-free children, follow Califano's advice: be a good example, keep prescription drugs out of reach, demand drug free schools, attend religious services with your children, have dinners together, and don't be wishy washy about letting the young people in your life know that drug use is either stupid or morally wrong, or both —whichever you think will work best with the child.

Resources:

Califano's website, the National Center on Addiction and Substance is surely the nation's gold standard for research on prevention and treatment. http://www.centeronaddiction.org.

You might find this part of the website particularly useful: http://www.centeronaddiction.org/addiction-research/reports/importance-of-family-dinners-2012. It gives details of why it's so important to have family meals together.

For a must-have book, get How to Raise a Drug-Free Kid: The Straight Dope for Parents – by Joseph A. Califano Jr.

High Society: How Substance Abuse Ravages America and What to Do About It 1st Edition
by Joseph A. Califano Jr.

CHAPTER 22

Security: Saving A World of Stress by Practicing Safe Cyber

Your family-owned business is likely to have a sophisticated plan for cyber security, so this is mainly about the vulnerabilities of your family members. You may find, as I have, that some members of your family are meticulously careful about avoiding malicious software –and some just haven't given it a thought.

I saw this recently when I was visiting my adored older sister at her home in New Hampshire in March of 2017. One morning, she came into the dining room where I happened to be working and casually said, "I've got a virus on my computer."

She saw the alarm on my face and quickly reassured me, "It's ok! This very nice guy is fixing it remotely. He said it would take about half an hour and then everything will be fine. He told me I'll soon be back on-line as if nothing had happened."

"How did you find out that you have a virus?"

"I got a flashing red sign on my screen," she answered. "The sign was really scary, and it warned that if I didn't call the number on the screen in five minutes, my computer would crash and I would permanently lose everything on my computer."

"WHAT!" I shrieked. "This is what ransom ware people do! We've got to turn off your laptop right now!"

"Oh no, I can't," she answered, still calm. "The guy told me not to touch the computer until he finished because otherwise..." here there was a flicker of doubt on her face, "...otherwise he wouldn't be able to fix it."

"Do you have anti-virus software installed," I asked with feelings of hope battling feelings of dread.

"Yes," she answered, and my hope meter went up, until she added, "but he helped me disable it so he could do the repairs."

A Ransom Ware Attack

At that moment, I knew this was a red alert, man-the-battle-stations, there's-in-coming situation. My sister didn't want me to do what I was about to do, but from what I had already heard, I knew we needed to stop "this very nice guy" from continuing to do his damage. I raced upstairs and disconnected her router from the Internet.

My sister still couldn't believe that there was something more serious going on. I was dreading to find out, but I had to ask. "Did he ask you to pay for his services?" I asked.

"Yes, his fee was $289."

"Did he ask for you to pay with a wire? Did he ask for your bank account number and router?"

"Yes, he told me that was the only way for him to get paid right now so he could start work."

"OMG," I answered, blood-pressure rising. "We've got

to get your bank account protected. Quick, let's call the bank!"

Unfortunately, this was during the worst blizzard of the year and no one at the bank was answering the phone.

Next, we tried to get into her bank's internet account so we could shut down the account and protect her assets. To our growing mutual horror, we discovered that her password had been changed, meaning that she was now locked out of her own account and now had no way to protect it. At this point, my darling sister realized that the situation was getting dire.

I'll say one thing: the guy acted fast.

The Consequences

It could have been a lot worse. At that exact moment, she didn't have a significant amount in her bank account, but she had recently sold some stock to pay taxes and a large amount was scheduled to be deposited in her compromised account the very next day.

When the bank opened that morning, we were there, waiting for the moment the doors opened. Under normal circumstances, I try to be a polite person and not be pushy, but I barged up to the manager's office and explained we had an emergency situation and I needed her attention *right now.*

I explained about the large deposit and the guy who had my sister's banking information, and the manager was kind enough to drop everything and close my sister's account instantly.

Phew!

Other good news was that we had disconnected from the Internet before "The very nice guy" got to freeze my sister's laptop. We preserved her essential files on an external hard drive and then took the laptop to the Geek Squad to do a clean install, removing everything and starting over again.

My sister had to open a new bank account, and she had to change every password, including the router's password, banking passwords, shopping passwords and on and on.

She didn't lose more than a couple of hundred dollars, but there was a price to be paid in both time and anxiety.

Backups to Protect Against Ransom Ware

To protect against ransom ware, keep full backups on external drives that are not connected to your computer. A hacker can't get at a disconnected drive.

Unfortunately, if the backup that you're counting on is connected to your computer at the time of the infection, it can quickly spread to your external hard drive.

You may not feel the need to do what I do, but I have eight external hard drives. Each has an entire backup of my system a week apart. I have external hard drives because some ransomware will infect your machine and then not activate for a couple of months. When you restore your data from a week-old backup hard drive, it could still have the same infection on it.

HOW TO MAKE YOUR FAMILY BUSINESS LAST

A Balance

In all things having to do with your personal security, there's a balance between spending too much time on precautions and being too lackadaisical. Only you know what the right balance is. For me, spending a couple of minutes a day (and it's not more) on backups and keeping software up-to-date is a small price for feeling protected from malware attacks.

Checklist for cyber security

Don't Get Taken in by Scary Messages such as, "You've been infected!!"
When a scary message comes up on your computer screen saying you've been infected with a virus and that you need to call the number on the screen immediately, be aware that this is a common entry point for malware, particularly ransomware. Don't get taken in and do not call the number on the screen.

Do not permit an unknown person to disable your anti-malware system and do not give out any valuable information.
Information never to give out includes (but is not limited to) passwords, banking information, social security number.

Be aware of "Dear User"
If you get a message from PayPal, eBay, any bank or other websites that says "Dear User," it is likely to be fake. Any legitimate website uses your first and last name when communicating with you.

Be cautious about social media. Consider never posting information on social media about where you are. I don't do it because this can give thieves information that you're away and it's safe to rob your home. Or if you're a woman and you've just posted, "I'm at the Pizza Parlor and will be home at 11:00 pm" a rapist could know where and when to be waiting for you. It's happened.

Double check any email that contains links or videos.
Don't follow links in any e-mail without checking with the sender that they really did send it. About one in five of the e-mails I get are to fraudulent links. Beware of opening videos unless you're confident that the material really is from the sender.

Be extremely cautious of .zip files.
They may look as if they're coming from FEDEX or someplace else that you trust, but they can contain viruses. According to the daily reports on my laptop that Trend Micro anti-virus software gives me, most of the zipped files that come into my in-box contain malware. *Good grief!*

When in doubt, try a hard reset.
Many computer viruses found on home routers, digital video recorders and cameras won't survive a hard reset. Turning your computer or other digital device off may solve your problem. If you're lucky.

Keep up with all security patches.

Use different passwords for all on-line accounts.

Avoid forwarding chain mail letters.
Usually the letter will instruct you to forward the e-mail to ten more people. Often these contain code that enables spam companies to harvest current e-mail addresses to sell to their customers. There are people who spend their working hours devising irresistible religious or political or charitable or humorous e-mails that you'll want to send to your friends. If you want to protect your friends from spam, don't forward these. Some of these are so well-done that it can be really tempting, but be aware that there's a good chance that their real purpose is address-harvesting.

Resources:

The Small Business Administration has its Top Ten Cybersecurity Tips. https://www.sba.gov/managing-business/cybersecurity/top-ten-cybersecurity-tips
The following site provides 131 cyber security tips. https://heimdalsecurity.com/blog/cyber-security-tips/. I don't do all of them, but I regularly comb through them to see where I might be vulnerable and what I should do about it.

CHAPTER 23

Personal Safety: Knowledge and Awareness Are Your Friends

Kidnappings are a danger for well-known families. Fortunately, there's a lot you can do to prevent becoming a victim and there's a lot to know about how to act if a kidnapping does occur.

The information you're about to read comes from conversations with Perdue Farms' retired Director of Security, Jim McCauley. The subject is an unpleasant one, and you're almost certain not to need this information. However, in the incalculably small chance that you do need it, the information could save the life of a loved one.

Kidnappings are Seldom Spontaneous

One of the first things to keep in mind is that a person or persons looking for a fast dollar seldom go about it in a spur-of-the-moment way. More usually, they'll have had the victim under surveillance to get an idea of their traffic patterns and when the individual would be most vulnerable. And by the way, the preferred victims are children, wives, and the elderly. Kidnappers want the individuals that are the easiest to control physically, and they also need someone left at home who can take charge and get them the funds that they are seeking.

Develop Situational Awareness

This doesn't mean obsessing about things, but if there's

something unusual, listen to your "Spidey sense." (This refers to the cartoon character Spider Man and his supposed ability to detect danger almost without thinking about it.)

What I'm about to describe is an unlikely situation, and it assumes that you are mentally healthy and not given to paranoia, but if you get the feeling that your home is being watched or that a vehicle is following you, pay attention.

I remember once noticing a guy across the street from the seven-story building where I live and he was watching my building. I made a mental note of it (my Spidey sense at work) and then, when I saw the guy still there half an hour later, I noticed him doubly and decided that in case I ever needed this information, I would make the effort to be able to describe him.

The next day there was a rash of burglaries in my building and one woman who had left her door open, was terrified to find the guy matching my description in her living room, going through her silver. I was able to give the police a fairly detailed description of the guy, and it matched what my neighbor had seen. This experience, of noticing the guy who seemed to be surveilling my building, strengthened my belief that our instincts can be worth paying attention to.

What if You're in a Dodgy Area and Have to Stop at a Traffic Light?

This seems like a small thing, but be sure you know where the "lock the doors" button is on your car. I remember once a bad guy came rushing at my car when I was stopped at a traffic light in a dicey neighborhood.

He lunged to open the door, but it was locked, and I gunned the car to get out of there. I still remember the utter consternation on his face when he realized the car was locked.

So, make sure that in any area that seems unsafe, that your doors are locked, and the windows up. If someone comes out of their car towards you, and your Spidey Sense is telling you, *"This is very not good,"* I wouldn't hesitate to go through a traffic light.

Another possibility is, you stop at the red light in a lonely neighborhood and then a stranger's car bumps into your back bumper. Your instinct is to get out and inspect the damage, but don't do it. Crack your window just enough to tell them, "We'll go up to the service station and talk about it." Even if you're injured, drive on to the nearest public place, like a gas station.

What About Dangers at Home?

At your house, a criminal may try to gain access under the pretext that they are lost or need directions or need help with their car. I have a second cousin who had a bad guy knock on her door in a suburban area, telling her that he needed a glass of water because his car engine had overheated and the water would somehow help.

She had a bad feeling about the person, but she didn't want to come across as uncaring to a person in need. She kept him outside, got the glass of water, and then opened the door a crack to hand him the glass of water.

Instead of taking the glass, he lunged with his shoulder as hard as he could against the door, burst in, grabbed a glass ink well and smashed at her head enough to require 38 stitches and then raped her and threatened to kill her infant girl. The trauma of this is going to last the rest of her life.

If a person unknown to you comes to the door, talk to them through the closed door. Do not allow strangers into your house. If they need assistance, tell them you'll make a phone call on their behalf. Don't be like my dear cousin who put being polite above her personal safety.

Other Places to be Alert

Parking lots can be an area for abductions. If a car has been following you and you see that vehicle parked by your car, don't go to your vehicle. Go back inside and seek assistance for someone to escort you out. Also write down the license number so you can provide it to law enforcement officials.

Also vans are sometimes used for abductions. They park beside your car, blocking the view of passersby, pull you in as you go to your car, shut the door and drive away.

What Should We Do if a Family Member is Abducted?

There's something critically important to know and keep in mind: *it is ALWAYS best to give the information to the local law enforcement immediately.* Abductors will tell you that it will end badly for the victim if you call for help, but in fact, if you try to negotiate with the abductors, you increase the odds of the situation ending in disaster.

Their goal is getting money and getting away, and they don't care about the hostage and they particularly don't want to leave a witness. They know that their chances of coming to trial without a witness are small so they'll do what it takes to get rid of any evidence that will link them to the crime. The chances of the hostage's surviving are vastly better if the police are involved.

The Phone Call, "We've Got Your husband." Or, "We've Got Your Child."

According to Jim McCauley, in a fair number of cases, it will be a bluff. Ask, "Is my husband alive? I'm not going to speak to you unless you show me that you have him and that he is alive."

Be sure you don't fall for the "Give me $40,000 at some corner in an hour" when they don't actually have him. They'll tell you things like that the hostage will be killed and you'll only find him in little pieces.

They're trying to make it sound as bad as they can make it in order to get you emotionally distraught. They place time restraints also, so you'll think that there's not a moment to spare to place the 911 call.

But let's suppose it's real and they do have your wife, child, or whoever. Again, according to McCauley, your most important job is to get as much information as you can from the kidnappers.

The kind of information you can get can save your loved one's life. Be calm and work to get information that the law enforcement professionals can use. If you have caller ID, write down the number. If you don't, use dial back immediately (*69 on your phone pad, if you have this service) after they hang up so you can get the number.

Law enforcement can then pinpoint where the call came from. Even if it's a pay phone, this information is critical.

Play along with the kidnappers and promise to get the money and not to involve the authorities. Get very clear directions on where the drop is.

And then call 911 as fast as you can. McCauley told me that law enforcement has a bunch of tricks that can thwart kidnappers and that aren't publicly known, and to repeat, it's always best to involve law enforcement instantly, no matter what the kidnappers say.

Checklist for Personal Safety

> **Have a plan.** In the extremely unlikely case that a family member is kidnapped, the plan should include calling the police no matter what the kidnappers threaten.
>
> **Insist on proof of life.** The kidnapper needs to demonstrate that the family member is alive. You don't want to fall victim to a bluff.
>
> **Develop situational awareness.** If you suspect you're being followed or monitored, pay attention. You probably aren't being followed, but it costs nothing to listen to your Spidey Sense. If a mall parking lot feels deserted and dangerous, ask the mall security to escort you to your car.
>
> **Develop the habit of locking your doors when you're in the car and have the windows up**

Do not allow strangers in your home no matter what their pretext. Through the closed door, you can offer to make a phone call for them if necessary. The problem here is, bad guys may try to use your kindness and generosity against you. They know you don't want to be unkind or rude, and bad guys regularly take advantage of how people who are nice have been socialized. Don't fall for this kind of manipulation.

Have a special "safe word" that indicates "be hyper aware." The "safe word" indicates that "Something super important is going on that I can't explain right now, but DO AS I SAY." For my son Carlos, the "safe word" was calling him "Charles," and for my son Jose, is was calling him, "Joe." Calling my sons by a name I'd never use under ordinary circumstances means, "Don't argue with me, do whatever I say, there's something really, really serious and dangerous going on." I've never had to use it but I think we all like knowing it's there.

Resource:

The Gift of Fear, Gavin de Becker, 2010. This book has had more than 2000 Amazon reviews, almost all of them five-star. I've often wondered how many lives this book has saved. De Becker's premise is, we need to listen to our inner voice when it's saying a situation is dangerous. In his experience, it's natural for us to try to talk ourselves out of our fears. However, he's seen too often that ignoring our instincts can land us in situations that could be somewhere between difficult and catastrophic.

SECTION III

PERDUE UNIVERSITY: (THE CHICKEN ONE, NOT THE UNIVERSITY IN INDIANA)

INTRODUCTION

Having a section on education in a book about making your family business last may seem an anomaly. But here's why I've done it, and why I hope you'll find it useful.

The more skills in the family's talent stack, the more approaches the family and the family business have available for solving problems. Everyone wins. Education strengthens the family.

The information you'll find here is different from what you'd find in a classroom. I have endless admiration for the kind of education someone might get from, for example, Indiana's Purdue University. However, what you'll find here in what I jokingly call My Own Personal Perdue University, is soft skills that you won't find in a classroom—unless I'm teaching it!

In the following section, you'll find here's-how-they-did-it advice based on how Father and Frank each built Fortune 500-size companies. I had the unique privilege as a daughter and a wife of observing things that set them apart and that contributed to their success. I also got to ask the people around them what Father and Frank did that others don't.

I think it may be a unique perspective on success. It's not the whole story of what it takes to be successful, but some

of the attitudes and approaches I got to witness haven't
been studied academically. To get the information you'll
read here takes someone who's on-the-scene and able to
observe the successful individuals over long periods of
time. I was able not only to question both men in real time,
I also got to question those around them.

I'll also be sharing some skills from my own background. I
was a syndicated television hostess, and for most of my
adult life I was also a syndicated columnist, first for
California's Capitol News and later for the Scripps Howard
News Service.

Communication skills can be a magic shortcut to influence.
These skills can magnify the family's prestige and benefit
the company's brand. They're also priceless for self-
confidence. And the wonderful thing is, in general,
communication skills don't cost you anything, except a lot
of practice.

Remember, the more skills your family members have, the
more they can contribute, not just to the family and the
family business, but also to the wider world. So, dear
friends, grow the family's talent stack! Strengthen the
family while at the same time being all you can be!

The more skills family members have, the better for the
family. I've coming up with a theory that it's a *Law of the
Universe* that when you learn a new skill, that somehow,
you'll find a use for the skill. In fact, you're likely enough
to find an actual *need* for the new skill.

I don't know why this happens. I've just seen that it does.

HOW TO MAKE YOUR FAMILY BUSINESS LAST

Whether I'm right on this theory or not, it's true that with more skills in the family's talent stack, there are more approaches available for solving problems. Everyone wins.

So, be winners! Grow the family's talent stack!

CHAPTER 24

Advice For Young People: Shut Up And Listen!

I recently had a conversation with Jack Tatem, a former Perdue Vice President, and learned some serious, if harsh, advice for young people. I worry that the advice may sound too harsh, but balancing that consideration, it's also exceptionally useful advice.

If you're a young person and you want to advance in your career, here's some golden advice from someone who has hired and supervised many hundreds of people:

"Shut up and listen!"

Tatem went on to say, "Most kids I run into today seem to think they already know it all. Frank Perdue was a one-of-a-kind genius, but even as successful as he was, he was always listening!"

Listen 90% of the Time, Talk 10% of the Time

Since I'm a writer, and part of my job is to observe things, I noticed something that was a constant in how Frank related to people. When he was interacting with anyone, he was listening 90% of the time and only talking 10% of the time.

And he didn't just listen, he frequently took notes about what he was hearing. He was an information-gathering machine.

When someone said something that he could act on, he'd write the information on one of the card-size sheets of notepaper he always carried in his breast pocket.

His handwriting was microscopic. If most people's handwriting is a font size 12, Frank's handwriting was a font size six. This meant he could usually fit six or seven of these notes on one sheet, which meant he'd typically have 40 or so actionable pieces of information in his pocket.

Act on What You've Heard

When we were in a taxi or waiting in the airport or any other moment of down time, he'd go through the notes and act on them. This could mean making a phone call or dictating a plan of action to his executive assistant, Elaine Barnes, or simply writing a note to the individual.

When he had acted on whatever piece of information he had heard, he'd draw a line through it and when all the items on that sheet of paper had lines drawn through them, he'd throw that sheet away.

Part of the reason for Frank Perdue's success is he listened. But he also made the most of his listening. He wrote down what he heard, followed up on it, and didn't stop until he had made use of what he had heard.

This technique of gathering information and then acting on it helped turn Frank into one of the world's most successful businessmen.

"Shut up and listen!" is good advice. It worked well for someone who made a success of himself.

Gathering information from everyone by listening and then acting on the information is a technique that can help you in your career. Try it!

Checklist for Effective Listening

Listen 90% of the time and talk 10% of the time.
Since none of us is as smart as all of us, we need to learn from others and listening is an excellent way to learn.

In addition to listening, Take notes.
Odds are without notes you can remember a few things, but with notes, you can remember all the things you need to remember.

Act on the notes.
Remember the old saying, "To know and not to act is the same as not to know."

CHAPTER 25

Winners' Tip: Ready, Fire, Aim!
(Yes, I Did Mean It In This Order)

Both my father and husband had a huge propensity for action. The agility they had in putting ideas into action resulted in a tremendous competitive advantage. With both men, being willing to act rapidly was a major ingredient in their success. It can by in yours as well.

I remember one night in the very early 1950s, my father told his family over dinner that he had decided to get into the credit card business. The Diner's Club Credit Card had just come into being, and Father shared his thinking about how that could be an opportunity for Sheraton.

He reasoned that as a national hotel chain with tens of thousands of customers in its database, Sheraton should get into this attractive new business. He told me with a pleasure that seemed almost boyish, "We thought about getting into it today, and we started working on it today!"

In a matter of weeks, Father rolled out Sheraton's own credit card. This agility proved profitable. He had created a large, fully functional credit card system which a few years later Sheraton sold to another credit card company for a small fortune. He had done in weeks what took our competitors more than a year.

I got to learn more than you might expect about credit cards. My first job at age 15 was as a file clerk for the Sheraton Credit card part of the business. I and eight other file clerks sat in a small office with shoe box-size containers filled with alphabetized credit cards. There were thousands of these boxes, and our job each day was to match credit cards with lists of people who had or hadn't paid their bills.

When people paid their hotel bills promptly, using the credit card, we'd know it and we'd raise their credit rating. For people who spent a lot and had a perfect record for payment, we had a code as part of the credit card's number that told the front desk people that they were dealing with a VIP.

However, for individuals who weren't paying their bills, the cards were yanked and people at the front desks of the hotels were given lists of credit card numbers not to accept. I was impressed that Father could come up, in such a short time, with such an elaborate plan for vetting the cards.

This meant that when he sold the credit card division of Sheraton, the cards had a lot of value because, after a couple of years, we knew about the spending habits and reliability of each card holder.

Agility: A Secret of Success

I often asked Father about his success, and what I just told you about how he got into the credit card business turned out to be emblematic of many of his answers. He felt that being able to respond rapidly and with agility gave him a huge advantage over competitors.

He said that he felt that part of his success came from being the first to introduce innovations. Some examples: he was the first to introduce air conditioning; he was the first to have bathroom scales; he even was the first to introduce the pull-out strings you could use to hang your socks over the bathtub, and he came up with that idea because it was something he wanted for himself and figured out that others would want it also.

I asked in the case of air conditioning back in the early 1950s why he went to the enormous expense of paying for this innovation. His answer was, he was sure that because of the demand for comfort, that it would be available everywhere soon.

That meant he'd have to pay for it anyway at some time to remain competitive. However, there's a lot of advertising and word-of-mouth value to being first. His attitude was, "If you're going to have to spend the same money either way, why not be first and get the benefit from it?

As he pointed out, you don't win a lot of points by advertising, "Look at us! We were third in introducing air conditioning!" No, it was the agility it took to be the first that meant the big payoff.

One of the Biggest Wastes, and Don't Do It!

His attitude was that doing 90 percent of what is required is one of the biggest wastes because you have nothing to show for it. But doing 110 percent of what is expected is one of the smartest investments because it can pay off with a big reputation for just a little more effort.

Frank Was Famous for Firsts

Frank was equally innovative. He was famous for being the first to advertising a commodity, but that was just the beginning.

- He was the first to star in his own commercials.

- He was a pioneer in avian genetics, having created broader breasted chickens

- He transformed food truck deliveries by going into the transportation business himself so he could control on-time delivery. (You know Perdue chickens, but we're also among the larger trucking companies.)

- He got into the grain business so he could control the quality of the feed for his chickens.

- He got into the oil seed business and you may be consuming some of Perdue vegetable oils in, for example, Little Debbie snacks, Frito Lay chips, and Stauffer cookies.

Frank loved to quote the story of an old sea captain who told his son, "My competition copies everything I do, but they can't copy my mind and I leave 'em huffing and puffing a mile and a half behind."

For Frank, the agility that resulted from research and development and the ability to put ideas into action were the magic keys to leaving competitors "huffing and puffing a mile and a half behind."

Both Frank and Father had a huge propensity to action. They might be willing to put immense amounts of research and study into something, but they weren't afraid to commit and "pull the trigger." They loved action.

And what about you? Be willing to "pull the trigger." And be willing to do it sooner than your competitors.

Checklist for Acting Rapidly

> **Remember the tremendous competitive advantages of being first**
>
> **Cultivate and reward the satisfaction of knowing that you can be more agile than the competitors**
>
> **Listen to your customers and win points with them by acting rapidly .**
>
> **Ask your line people for ideas** (Frank and now Jim always did this.)
>
> **Think about how to encourage, reward, and celebrate agility?**

CHAPTER 26

Technique for Being an Inspirational Leader: Give People a Better Vision of Themselves

There's something my father did that helped build the Sheraton hotels from one hotel to more than 100 during his lifetime. It's something you can do, and it's something that when I tell the story during a speaking engagement, I often see people taking notes on. I'm assuming they do this because it's useful information,

Here it is.

Father Created for People a Better Vision of Themselves

What I'm about to describe happened in the 1930s. When Father would take over a hotel, usually one that had gone into bankruptcy because of the Great Depression, he'd make the hotel wildly popular and profitable.

He regularly could get this done in less than two years.

However, during the Great Depression, this kind of success in the hotel business was unheard of. Other hotels were going bankrupt right and left.

Here's how he did it.

On the day he assumed management of a hotel, he'd start by assembling the hotel's entire workforce in the hotel's ballroom. They'd be a demoralized group, each of them worrying that the new management would want to do some "house cleaning." That is, they'd be worried that they were about to lose their jobs.

161

After all, if a hotel was in severe financial straits, wouldn't it be reasonable to believe that the employees were at least partly responsible? And needed to go?

Father's reaction was the opposite. He told them at this first meeting that all of them were going to keep their jobs. He told them that they knew the hotel better than anyone else, and he viewed his job as making it possible for them to show just how good they were.

He'd also tell them that he knew the future success of the hotel depended on them and they were now on a winning team with a bright future. He'd finish by telling them that he believed in them.

Then, beginning that day, he'd start backing up his words with actions. Part of a hotel turnaround always had to involve refurbishing the guest rooms and public rooms. That, however, was never where Father first invested money when taking over a hotel.

No, it was in refurbishing areas that the public would never see, such as the employee locker rooms or dining rooms or showers. It would mean modernizing the kitchens and laundry rooms and it would even mean making the stairs and elevators that the employees used nicer than they were before.

He had his top decorator, Mary Kennedy, pay attention to the decor of the employee areas before she went about renovating the guest rooms. Of course, the employees knew all this.

Define a New Reality
It was a powerful signal to the employees, one of many they'd experience throughout their time at Sheraton. Father

let them know that he valued their contribution and knew that they were the ones who could make the hotels a success.

He often told me that people want to live up to a leader's expectations, and since he demonstrated that he believed in them, they typically stayed with him for life. They performed far better than they ever had before, and hotels that had been failing often turned into the most popular hotel in the area.

Father's "secret sauce" was believing in people and having them buy into his vision. He was defining a new reality for them.

Why This Worked

In the story you just read about what my father did when taking over a hotel, step back with me for a moment and take a look at why this worked. When taking over a hotel and meeting with his new employees, he had a choice. He could have used soft or hard persuasion tactics.

If he was going to use the hard approach, he could have stood there on the stage of the ballroom of his newly acquired hotel and told everyone that they needed to shape up or be fired. That would be hard persuasion tactics and it would breed resentment, and although he could get compliance, he wouldn't be getting life-long commitment.

Instead, he used the soft tactic of offering them a better vision of themselves. He used inspiration. It boils down to "Inspire, don't require." Inspiration means that they internalized his view of the world. They internalized a better vision of themselves, and the hotel prospered.

HOW TO MAKE YOUR FAMILY BUSINESS LAST

Checklist for Getting Commitment

> **Be conscious of whether you're using the hard tactics of using an ultimatum, or the soft tactics of inspiration.**
> Hard tactics may get you compliance, as in short-term they'll grudgingly do what you require. In contrast, soft tactics can mean they endorse and internalize your vision and will do whatever they can to live up to it.

> **Be aware that loyalty is a two-way street.**
> One of the all-time powerful principles of persuasion is reciprocity. If you go out of your way to treat the people who work for you with respect, decency, and fairness, they're far more likely to go out of their way to help you.

Resources:

For an unending series of useful and inspiring ideas on employee engagement and leadership visit Skip Prichard at http://www.skipprichard.com . I've subscribed to his newsletter and follow him on Twitter as well.

Influence, the Psychology of Persuasion, Robert B. Cialdini. This is a classic, one that I read over and over again.

Influence: Mastering Life's Most Powerful Skill, Kenneth G. Brown, The Great courses. http://www.thegreatcourses.com/courses/influenc e-mastering-life-s-most-powerful-skill.html. I owe a large debt to Dr. Brown for showing me a new lens through which I can view my late father's actions.

CHAPTER 27

How to Get People to Share Your Vision

Getting people to see things your way is one of the most important ingredients in leadership. When you have this skill, people can become so committed to your vision that they'll work hard to make you and your projects a success. People will want to be on your team for life.

Frank Perdue was a master at persuading people to adopt his vision. Being able to do this was one of the biggest reasons he was able to grow a small chicken operation on Maryland's Eastern Shore to a company that today sells its products in almost 100 different countries.

Having people ready to follow him also helps account for his growing a father-and-son operation to one that today employs more than 20,000 people. An astonishing number of people stayed with him their entire careers, and those same people were usually ready to go the extra mile for him.

What are these leadership skills? And how can you use them? Interestingly, they're not difficult and they don't cost a penny. But you do need to know them and then act on them.

Make People Feel Important

The key to how much people want to follow you is how you make them feel about themselves. People will live up to—or live down to—what you think of them. Make people feel valued, trusted, and important and they'll tend to want to live up to your view of them.

Frank was constantly on the lookout for ways he could show his respect and appreciation for the people who worked with him. He knew the names of many thousands of the people who worked at the plants or the farmers who grew the chickens.

He even went so far, with my eager participation, as to entertain tens of thousands of Perdue associates for dinner, 100 at a time, in our own home. We did this several times a month for almost seventeen years, and he made sure that every guest felt appreciated, valued, and recognized.

He'd even serve his employees from behind the buffet line. (How many heads of Fortune 500 size companies would do that?) He was always on the lookout for ways of making people feel important.

Listen

This means full-on total attention. I've mentioned this before in the chapter that begins on Page 153, Advice to Young People: Shut Up and Listen! But, this is good advice for everyone.

The "this person-is-the-most-important-person-in-my-world-right-now" kind of attention makes people feel important and valued. When Frank was listening to you, it was as if there was no one else in the room and that you were all-important to him.

This kind of attention isn't quite the same thing as saying, "I love you," but, honestly, I think it's way up there.

And when he was listening, something important, his body language didn't overpower and "use up all the oxygen." When listening to you, his body language was different from what you might expect from a powerful CEO.

You didn't see the large dominating gestures of the flamboyant, powerful extrovert. Instead, his gestures tended to be small, more like talking with a teammate than with the Big Boss. The result was, you probably felt comfortable talking with him about your ideas.

Calibrate Your Appreciation

Frank wasn't effusive in his appreciation, but he calibrated it to what fit the individual. He understood when a big public celebration was what an individual craved, or when another individual might prefer something more private and personal.

I've heard people say that when Frank wrote, for example, a personal note of appreciation, that they'd keep that note for life. Or when he praised you to your face, you felt ten feet tall. My favorite example of calibrating individual recognition was when one associate, Owen Schweers, had worked for many months redesigning the boxes used for shipping product to market.

It was genius because with the new configuration, we could load more boxes per truck, which translates into savings in fuel and time. By saving on fuel, it would have been more environmental.

Unfortunately, the people on the receiving end didn't like the new boxes and the design had to be withdrawn. Frank, understanding the designer's intense disappointment, arranged for a tongue-in-cheek celebration with a real bronze plaque signed by the board of directors, awarding e

Schweers "The Great Failed Project Award." That happened decades ago, but the man still talks about it.

Encourage Others to Have Ownership.
When Frank wanted a problem solved, he wasn't into micro managing the solution. Instead, his default approach was to explore whatever the problem was with the team in charge of solving it.

He would tell them what results he was looking for, but he encouraged the others to figure out innovative ways to get there. They owned the project, including the solution and its implementation. By following this approach, he made his employees feel competent, valued, important, and most of all, engaged.

Show Respect.
I often heard him say that he wasn't all that smart, but as he'd go on to say, "I have the good fortune to be surrounded by smart people." And far from being a know-it-all, when he entered a room for a meeting, instead of telling people what to do, he was more likely to have the attitude that, "There's a lot of brainpower in this room, and I want to tap into all of it!"

Earn Respect.
Frank worked harder than anyone, studied harder than anyone, and made more sacrifices than anyone. People knew it and respected him for it.

Cherish the People Who Stand Up to You.
This is so important I devoted an entire chapter to it. See page 171 -- Seeking Out Diverse Viewpoints.

Frank gave people the respect of valuing their opinions, even when they were negative. Frank might argue with you, but if you could convince him you were right, he'd change his mind.

People who did well in the company were almost always the ones who would stand up to Frank and tell him the things he needed to hear. He showed them that he valued their points of view, even when (or maybe I should say "especially when") their views strongly differed from his own.

His willingness to take other points of seriously increased people's sense of engagement. And by the way, the man who argued with him most vociferously, who even snarled at him one day, "You should retire and take up hang gliding," was the man whom he later chose to become president of the company.

Be An Egalitarian.
I've watched Frank with the President of the United States and with factory workers on the line, and he treated them all with equal respect. When walking on the line, I noticed that he never had the attitude of, "I'm the big boss." Rather it was, "We're all a team, and while I have my role, I very much respect and value your role." People felt part of a team.

Developing this kind of inspirational approach to leadership is a soft skill, but it's one that can be learned. The rewards of having people stay with a company for life and being willing to go the extra mile for the company is one of the most valuable skills that you can learn.

Checklist for Creating Loyalty

Make people feel important.

HOW TO MAKE YOUR FAMILY BUSINESS LAST

Listen

Calibrate your appreciation

Encourage others to take ownership

Show respect

Earn Respect

Cherish the people who stand up to you

Be an egalitarian

CHAPTER 28

SEEKING OUT DIVERSE VIEW POINTS: A MASTER KEY TO SUCCESS

Frank Perdue had an attitude that I rarely see in others, but it's part of what made him a success. It's something that can contribute mightily to your success. Frank was more interested in criticism that flattery, and he had no use for "yes men."

The person who argued the most with Frank was the man Frank eventually appointed to succeed him as president of his company. This would have greatly surprised any outsider who didn't understand how Frank operated.

The Man Who Stood Up to Frank Most Was the Man Frank Chose to Succeed Him

Frank Perdue would have seemingly horrendous public arguments with the man in question, Don Mabe. As an example, Frank had once assembled a meeting with six sales people whom he, for unknown reasons, had nicknamed, "The Booger Bears."

One day the Booger Bears where in a small room, sitting along the sides of a conference table. Mabe and Frank were sitting at opposite ends of the table.

They may have been at opposite ends of the conference table, but they were also at opposite ends in their thinking. Mabe was a cost-conscious realist while Frank was more of a spend-what-it takes visionary.

HOW TO MAKE YOUR FAMILY BUSINESS LAST

Mabe had his eye on solvency and Frank's approach was, "You've get to spend money to make money." Mabe and Frank were Yin and Yang when it came to spending.

In the case I'm about to share with you, Frank and Mabe had been fighting like cats and dogs all day about whether to scrap the Cornish hen program. Mabe felt the program was too expensive.

Frank, on the other hand, wanted market share. At one point Don Mabe got so mad that he took his glasses off, and hurled them down hard on the conference table - with the result that the glasses bounced once and ended up hitting Frank square in the chest!

The salespeople who were there reported that the incident was so intense that it seemed to be happening in slow motion. Some were even having trouble breathing.

"Damn it, Frank," Mabe yelled at Frank, "You need to retire! Why don't you take up hang gliding!"

Frank picked up Don Mabe's reading glasses, calmly handed them to the guy next to him, who handed them to the guy next to him until the reading glasses got back to Mabe. Meanwhile the argument continued to rage.

Think about this for a moment: how many employers would be OK with a subordinate suggesting that his boss retire and take up a possibly life-threatening hobby? After throwing an object that ended up hitting the boss?

You'd think an incident like that would be the end of Mabe's and Frank's relationship, but in fact, Frank was fine with it. Frank and I had dinner with Don Mabe and his wife, Flo, soon after and we were all laughing about it.

Frank never held a grudge and deeply appreciated Mabe's views.

Mabe didn't win that battle, but he often got Frank to see his way. And further, Frank wasn't upset that Mabe expressed himself strongly: Frank put immense value on the fact that Mabe really, really cared.

Benefits from Cherishing Dissent

Frank knew that he benefited greatly by having someone confront him with the other side of important questions. This was a pattern that Frank followed regularly: he valued the people who stood up to him; he never held it against them; and he deeply appreciated that they cared more about doing the right thing than about telling the boss what he might want to hear.

When people focused on doing and saying what they believed was right, as opposed to sucking up to the boss, there were two priceless results:

- The people who stood up to him had ownership of their ideas. They weren't twisting into a pretzel to accommodate ideas they didn't believe in. Being authentic translates into deepened engagement.

- Frank was the recipient of better ideas when people felt free to disagree with him.

In your own career, consider taking to heart Frank's attitude that "None of is as smart as all of us." For better decisions and more employee engagement, cherish dissent.

HOW TO MAKE YOUR FAMILY BUSINESS LAST

Checklist for Appreciating Dissent

Do you see the value of opposing viewpoints?

Can you keep from holding a grudge when someone in the company argues with you?

Can you see past the argument and how it's expressed to the fact that by arguing with you, the person is showing the he or she really cares and is deeply engaged and committed?

Can you prove by your actions that being surrounded by yes men is something you neither want nor will reward?

CHAPTER 29

BE THE PERSON OTHER PEOPLE WANT TO DO BUSINESS WITH

How did the Sheraton Hotel Chain grow from an investment of just $1,000 to an international behemoth at the time of my father's death in 1967?

Here's the story, and it involves a principle that might work for you. It centers on being the kind of person people want to do business with.

My father, his brother, and his college roommate received war bonuses after their military service in World War I that totaled $1000 for the three of them.

They decided to pool their resources to go into business together, and the result was an international company that grew so explosively that by the time of my father's death, their company employed 20,000 people and was worth close to $1 billion in 1967 dollars.

People often ask me the secret for Sheraton's spectacular growth. That's exactly the question I often asked my father.

Develop A Reputation for Being Both Fair and Generous

He had several answers to this question, but one of the answers that stands out most in my mind is, he said it was a tremendous advantage to have a reputation for being fair.

HOW TO MAKE YOUR FAMILY BUSINESS LAST

People want to do business with people they can trust, people who will do what they say they're going to do.

Part of his approach to being fair included a negotiating style that was generous. He made it a practice to "leave something on the table."

What he meant by this phrase was, he wouldn't drive the hardest bargain he could. In fact, he felt that it wasn't a good deal unless both sides were enthusiastic about it. He contrasted this to "the sharks" who entered a bargaining session with the goal of winning every last penny.

This approach may have been one of the bigger factors in the growth of Sheraton. A lot of Sheraton's growth came about because when someone wanted to sell a hotel, Father would find that Sheraton was the first company that the individual had offered the property to.

The reason? The individuals (or their lawyers) knew that they'd be treated fairly - even generously. Hotel sales often came about because a widow or the children didn't want to run a hotel that they had inherited, and when it came to selling it, they didn't want to be taken advantage of.

My father's view about "leaving something on the table," meant he don't make as much as he could on each individual deal, but he made up for this dozens of times over when sellers come to him first. He ended up having the pick of the best properties before they were offered elsewhere.

People want to do business with people who are fair. People want to do business with people they like and trust and who have a reputation for doing what they'll say they'll do. This reputation may not pay off immediately, but over time, it can mean that you get the first offers and the best offers.

Checklist for Being the Kind of Person Others Want to Do Business With

> In negotiations, be willing to leave something on the table.

> Don't drive the hardest bargain possible.

> Do what you say you'll do, so you develop a reputation for being trustworthy.

> Keep in mind that you're playing a long game, one where reputations are built over decades.

CHAPTER 30

HOW TO EAT AN ELEPHANT: SIX STEPS TO SOLVING MOST PROBLEMS

Something that I've observed about the most successful people I've known: they solve problems.

Sometimes they may need to think about the problem for a while, but they don't stare at it and wish it would go away.

For myself, I have a stock way of dealing with most problems and it involves six steps. The biggest key to my system is breaking the problem into its components and then dealing with the smaller components.

It's the old, "How do you eat an elephant?"

"One bite at a time."

For me getting things done involves breaking the big problem into bite-size fairly-easy-to-accomplish smaller tasks. I make lists of the small tasks and then mark the tasks off with "DONE" for each step that I've completed.

Somehow, watching those "DONE"s accumulate next to the tasks feels encouraging. It gives a feeling of momentum.

The Steps:

1. **Describe the Problem**.
   Preferably do this in writing. The act of putting the problem into words can clarify your thinking. I can't count the number of times that simply

explaining the problem enables me to see the solution. But not always, so if that doesn't make the situation clear, go on to #2.

2. **Write Down the Obstacles**.
   Although I'm a fan of positive thinking, I'm also a believer in Dr. Ellen Galinsky's research. She's the author of *What Every Child Should Know*, and her research shows that no matter how positively you think about a problem, you're less likely to get the results you want if you don't match your optimism with realistic examination of the obstacles.

3. **Brainstorm Possible Solutions**.
   Think of as many solutions as you can. At this point, the goal is quantity not quality. That's because bad ideas may spark your imagination and lead to good ideas that you wouldn't have thought of otherwise.

4. **Stretch to Find One More Solution.**
   Ideas that come when you've had to stretch for them often turn out to be the most useful. There's a reason: In many cases if the answer were easy or obvious, it would already have been done by now. It's when you stretch to get a new idea that you come up with the most creative ideas, the ones that not everyone has already thought of. The most creative, least obvious ones may have the best chance of solving your problem. Oh, and something to keep in mind at this point: Thomas Edison was right: "When you have exhausted all possibilities, remember this: you haven't."

5. **Pick the Best Solution.**
   Now is the time to put on your realist's hat. Of all

the ideas you've come up with, choose which best meets the criteria not only of solving the problem, but getting the job done in the right timeframe and with the resources that you can put your hands on.

6. **Act on it.**
   The people I know who are most successful have a penchant for action. They're not only good at thinking of solutions; they're very good at plunging in and doing them.

Three quotes that express the importance of action:

- "To know and not to act is the same as not to know."

- "It's not what you know, it's what you do."

- "Done is better than perfect."

Checklist for Solving Problems

Have I described my problem in writing?

Have I made a clear assessment of the obstacles?

Have I brainstormed solutions?

Have I stretched to find one more solution?

Have I picked the best solution?

Have I put the solution into action?

CHAPTER 31

BE AN INFORMAVORE: IT'S SOMETHING MEGA SUCCESSFUL PEOPLE DO

Both Frank Perdue and Ernest Henderson each attributed much of their success to being willing to see things in new ways. But what was the source of their creativity?

And more importantly, can you harness their approach to creativity? (I'll tell you ahead of time, the answer, is yes.)

Both men were extreme *informavores*. (That's a made-up word. An informavore devours information the way a carnivore devours meat.)

By endlessly accumulating knowledge on amazingly different subjects, they could see connections invisible to others. I have a favorite story of the lengths my father would go to do that.

Father Went Out of His Way to Get Good Ideas

One day in the 1950s, Father drove from Boston to a small town in upstate New Hampshire to hear a lecture on business. I knew it was an all-day journey, traveling on crummy roads.

I also learned later that the people attending were local businessmen and women, including the owner of a local gas station and a small-town grocery store—and here joining them was the president of a national hotel chain that employed 20,000 people.

That night at the dinner table, he described his day. What I was hearing seemed incongruous to me. I think I was only maybe 13 years old, but I challenged him: "These aren't the Big Wigs you could be hanging out with. Why did you go?"

I'll never forget his answer. "When you get one good idea, it can change your life." He went on to say that the subject interested him, the speaker was an authority, and he felt it was time well spent.

Father was the head of a New York Stock Exchange-listed company, but he wasn't above hanging out with mom and pop business owners if the subject interested him. He told me, "Having access to good ideas gives me a leg up on the competition!"

Frank Went to Extremes to Get Good Ideas

Frank was equally an informavore. He was always reading, and the topics that interested him were diverse. He knew enough about Empress Catherine the Great to have a lively discussion about her with the Librarian of Congress; he knew enough about Alexander Hamilton so that the docent of the Hamilton Museum in Nevis ended up asking Frank about Hamilton as if he were the docent when we toured the museum there; and you wouldn't believe how much Frank Perdue knew about treasure hunting.

I've even seen him dazzle generals with his knowledge of military history. Or you could catch him discussing the latest John Grisham novel with one of his good friends, a local judge. When a subject interested Frank, he would dive into it.

HOW TO MAKE YOUR FAMILY BUSINESS LAST

Of course he applied this intensity to business. When he wanted to get into advertising, he took a ten weeks' absence from running his company, went to New York and went through a self-directed total immersion, full-time study of the theory and practice of advertising. One of his first steps was joining the Association of National Advertisers, so he could access their library.

In addition to reading books and papers on advertising, he talked with the sales managers of every newspaper, and radio and television station in the New York area. He also created a grid on a map of the food stores that might purchase Perdue chicken, and talked with hundreds of these potential buyers about what they wanted to hear about chicken.

When it came to selecting an ad agency, he interviewed sixty-six agencies, and from those, narrowed the selection to six.

This was typical of every decision he made (except for marrying me). The research he put into making decisions is legendary.

So, dear friends, this tip for being a winner is: *be an informavore*. Fill your internal databanks with enormous amounts of information. Widen your aperture and bring in a broader range of data. Have no limit to your curiosity.

To repeat what my late father said, "One idea can change your life." So, unendingly put yourself in the way of finding good ideas. One good idea can change your life, and dozens of good ideas can make you successful on a scale you didn't dream.

HOW TO MAKE YOUR FAMILY BUSINESS LAST

Checklist for Getting Information

Read everything. It doesn't have to be disciplined reading. It's better if it isn't because you never know where you'll find a good idea or make some connection between ideas that hasn't occurred to anyone else.

Attend lectures every chance you get.

Go to conferences and conventions

Network with people whose work is related to your field

Invite people in your field to lunch and pick their brains. There's a good chance they'll enjoy it because it's flattering when someone wants to learn from you.

Take classes I make it a rule to take at least one class a year.

Invest in coaching sessions

Join associations

Haunt the Internet.

Set up Google alerts on a topic

Sign up for newsletters

Listen to podcasts

Join a mastermind group

Talk with people. If you're at a dinner party or on a plane or train or bus, talk with people. Find out their concerns and ways of looking at things.

CHAPTER 32

LEARN HOW TO WORK A ROOM: MOST PEOPLE DON'T KNOW HOW

Businessmen typically go to big public events for several reasons, but at least one of these reasons is networking. If it's a charitable or political event, they're also there to be visibly supportive of whatever the cause is.

However, after investing the time and the money to be there, how many people make a study of how best to accomplish their networking and visibility goals?

Frank did.

How to Accomplish Your Networking and Visibility Goals

I used to watch in awe, as he'd work a room with a politician's skill. When we'd go to an event, I'd notice that at the end of it, we had talked with just about everyone there.

Each contact may have been brief, but he made the effort to look the individual in the eye, shake his or her hand, and for a moment, give the person the feeling that they were the most important person in his world.

If you were shaking hands with him, you probably felt enveloped by his attention. The rest of the world didn't exist for him, and if he asked you a question, which typically he would, he'd listen to your answer.

I mentioned a moment ago that at the end of an event, we'd have shaken hands and spoken with almost everyone in the room. Interestingly, this didn't happen by accident.

Arrive Early

Frank made it a rule always to arrive at the very beginning of an event, or most often a moment before. For example, if the invitation to a reception was for 6:00 PM, we would be there at 5:59 PM. (You do know, don't you, how legendarily prompt he was?)

He'd position himself inside the room but close enough to the entrance so he could interact with the maximum number of people as they came in. Being there at the beginning of the event and positioning himself near the entrance meant that in a deliberate and organized way, he had a chance to interact with virtually everyone who attended.

Plan for Follow Up

Something else that he was forever doing at these events. He exchanged business cards the way everyone else does, but in addition, he would often take notes about conversations. He'd be doing this in real time.

If someone said something that he needed to follow up on, he'd take out one of the little cards he kept in his breast pocket and make notes on what he needed to pursue.

It might be a complaint about his product or a business opportunity—or who knows. But the important thing is, he took notes right then and there. He didn't leave it to chance if he would remember later the 20 or so action opportunities that came from his networking.

By the way, he invariably acted on his notes. Typically, the note would take up a couple of lines on the card and there would be four or more additional action items also on that card. Those cards stayed in his pocket until he had acted on every point on the card.

Frank Perdue was a master at working a room. He understood that for his brand, he needed to be visible so he deliberately positioned himself where he could talk with most of the people attending an event. He also made the effort to listen and make the other person feel important by encouraging him or her to do most of the talking.

You can do the same.

Checklist for Working a Room

> **Make up your mind to take full advantage of networking opportunities.**
> Don't leave it to chance.

> **Arrive at the beginning of the event, or even a moment early.**

> **Position yourself near the front.**
> That way you can meet as many people as possible.

> **Pay 100% attention.**
> When you're talking with someone, even if only briefly, pay 100% attention to him or her. No looking over their shoulder to see if there's someone more interesting.

> **Ask a question and then listen to the answer.**

> **Take notes on possible action items.**

> **Act on the notes.**

CHAPTER 33

BE LIKEABLE: THE MAGIC
KEY TO INFLUENCE

Having the skill to make yourself likeable is priceless in all aspects of life, but this is particularly true in business. According to the legendary author of *Influence*, Dr. Robert Cialdini, "The people most likely to buy from you are people who like you."

They're also more likely to listen to you, to believe you and to be willing to look at the world the way you do. Frank understood this and simply made himself not only learn the social skills, but he practiced them, and in the end, perfected them.

Today, I think almost anyone who knew Frank Perdue would agree that he was world class at just about every aspect of socializing. Could you learn the social skills that can magnify your influence?

I think you can. After all, Frank didn't start out with these skills.

He grew up an only child on a farm. He told me that at school, he almost never participated in after-school activities, but instead would run home to help with chores.

Even in his 20s, when his father assigned him a job selling seed corn, he began his career being so shy that he was incapable of looking a prospect in the eye. How did this shy only child manage to transform himself into a legendary charmer?

189

HOW TO MAKE YOUR FAMILY BUSINESS LAST

Frank Made Himself Learn Social Skills

Frank really did master the art. I often meet people today who remember even a brief contact with Frank with exceptional pleasure. These include: a secretary in an office where Frank was visiting her boss and took the time to be pleasant and make her feel important; or a taxi driver who for the rest of his life remembered the pleasure of having Frank Perdue in his cab; or a server at a restaurant who remembered Frank treating him with the dignity of an equal.

One of the clues as to how he did this was his motto: "Treat all people with courtesy and respect, no exceptions."

I've said this before, but it's key: Frank made each person feel that he or she was important in Frank's world. Whether it was the President of the United States or an associate in one of the plants, he gave that person his total focus.

I think it would be fair to say of Frank Perdue that he never met anyone who was unimportant to him.

Be Unendingly Gracious

Being nice to everyone must have been at times a chore. But he never, ever showed it. Something that makes Frank unusual among celebrities: he was always gracious to autograph-seekers, no matter how much they were interrupting.

Because he was so famous, people were constantly coming up to him asking for his autograph.

Sometimes, for example, at an airport, he might have 20 people clamoring for his signature.

Or even when we were eating a quiet, romantic dinner in a secluded restaurant, people would interrupt, us, first to inform him, "You're Frank Perdue!" and second, to ask if they could have his autograph. For a lesser person, this could have gotten real old, real fast.

But not for Frank, or at least not that he ever let on. No matter what, he was gracious to all and would give them his patented "You're the most important person in the world to me at this moment" look.

Being gracious to just about everyone he came across was sincerely important to him. I remember once at a Shorebirds baseball game, the stadium's management was giving out bobble heads of Frank.

The line of people wanting Frank to autograph the Frank Perdue bobble head was at least two hours long. Since he already had Parkinson's disease, sitting still and signing autographs for that long was a serious, serious hardship for him.

Sensing that signing so many autographs was exhausting for Frank, officials from the Stadium several times told us that they were going to cut the line off and end the signing. Frank's response was that if people had waited so long to get the autograph, he wasn't going to disappoint them.

He insisted on signing autographs until the last person in line got one. (I'm pretty sure you've guessed before reading this that Frank was my hero. Actions like what I've just described are one of the reasons.)

Something else: he was a big believer in being self-deprecating. I remember once he counseled me not to talk about European vacations we had taken or fancy parties that we had attended because it might make the person I was talking with feel less important.

And another thing, he was the smartest man I'll ever meet, but he didn't let you know it. He was the most philanthropic person I'll ever meet, but he did his best to keep it hidden. He was a powerful man, and a financially successful man, but again, he never let any of that keep him from treating people as equals.

In his posture and his tone of voice and the words he used, he would be on the level of the person he was talking with. He could have had all sorts or airs, but he didn't. He never acted as if he were important. No, everything about him was focused on making you feel important.

I have a favorite quote from Cavett Roberts, the late founder of the National Speakers Association. Roberts said, "Everybody has a big sign on them that says, 'Make me feel important!'" Somehow Frank intuitively understood this concept, and it was a big part of what made him likeable.

Why Did Frank Do It?

What was behind Frank's learning to be good at socializing and making the effort to do it? Why would an innately shy person go to the trouble of perfecting and using this skill to such a degree that people remember his talent even decades later?

I don't know for sure, but I have some guesses. I think part of the well- spring of this was the same thing that made him visit the sick every weekend or always to attend funerals.

He had what was for me, unfathomable and almost incomprehensible, generosity of spirit.

Also, it probably made business sense, to behave so that as many people as possible would have a favorable opinion of him and thus, perhaps, a favorable opinion of his product.

Or maybe it was a skill that he wanted to master the same way he wanted to be good at ping pong or tennis.

However, my best guess is that he simply felt that treating everyone with decency and respect was the right thing to do. And he had to learn and hone and practice his people skills to do it.

The techniques he used are available to you.

Checklist for Social Skills

> **Care about people.**
>
> **Listen to them.**
>
> **Make them feel important.**
>
> **Don't decrease their feelings of importance.** Don't show that you are smarter, richer, better traveled or anything else that would make them feel less important.
>
> **Treat all people with courtesy and respect, no exceptions.**
>
> **Have the attitude that each person you're with is, at this moment the most important person in your universe.**

CHAPTER 34

COMMUNICATION: YOUR OWN
PERSONAL SUPERPOWER

David Grossman, author of *No Cape Needed*, looks on the ability to communicate as a superpower, and I agree. As he points out, "You can use communication to make others feel good about their jobs, to be engaged and excited, to help someone who's having a hard time get through a rough patch, or to inspire a team."

In addition, learning communication skills is a shortcut to success and influence. It gives your ideas visibility, and it's valuable for your family business's brand.

But What If You Feel You Have No Talent for Communicating?

Ah, dear friend, welcome to my world! Today I'm a professional writer and speaker, but I didn't start out that way. I got into writing when I felt I was about to lose my rice farm, and no one was telling my side of the story.

I had invested my inheritance and the inheritance of my two children in rice farming in Northern California. It was doing well, but in 1979, legislation was pending that would have put me and my fellow rice growers out of business.

I felt that the legislation was misguided. Even though I had zero experience with writing and hadn't even taken an English course in college, I felt that my only hope of saving my business was publicly communicating the rice grower's side of the issue.

HOW TO MAKE YOUR FAMILY BUSINESS LAST

I went to the local library and checked out, *How to Write Magazine Articles that Sell.* I followed it like paint-by-numbers. When it said, "Write a topic sentence," I wrote a topic sentence. When it said, "Develop an exciting opening," I worked to do that.

I had no writing experience whatsoever, but by following good advice on writing, I got my article published in one of the in-flight magazines for the major airline that serviced Sacramento. I had targeted this particular outlet because I wanted legislators to read why they shouldn't ban rice growing.

It became required reading for the California State Legislature. To my unending delight (I still feel happy when I think of it almost four decades later), once the public knew the other side of the story, the legislation got withdrawn.

Having discovered the incredible power of communication, I fell in love with writing. I began reading everything I could find on how to be a good writer. Eventually this lead to becoming a syndicated columnist.

But I don't think it was because I was an innately gifted writer. Rather, I was willing to follow good advice. My own view of my writing is, I'm a good, solid, journeyman writer, but maybe that's all you need.

I'm telling you all this because I'm certain that if you want to learn to be a writer, you can do it.

And as for speaking, good Lord, if I could do it, I think anyone can learn. Actually, I have more than 2,500 good reasons for believing that anyone can be a public speaker, and I'll get to them in the next chapter.

HOW TO MAKE YOUR FAMILY BUSINESS LAST

That's how many people I coached during my time as at television hostess. I had only 15 minutes in the CBS station in Sacramento to warm up my guests, and I developed some techniques that transformed people who were terrified into competent, interesting guests.

Ah, but that's for the chapter after this one.

Back to me and speaking. I think I was among the least likely persons ever to be a public speaker. I had a genuine phobia of public speaking, the equivalent to someone else's phobia of snakes or spiders.

Oh, and up until almost my 40s, I was so shy that it was horrendously difficult for me to enter a room of strangers. I was even so shy that back then that it was difficult for me to use the telephone.

What bothered me back then was I wasn't sure I'd know what to say, and there were times when I could sit on the edge of my bed and take ten minutes practicing what I was going to say and then imagining how I'd answer whatever was said on the other end of the line.

How did I change from being *that* shy to someone who enjoys few things more than being on camera or on stage? How did I change into someone who looks forward to giving a talk the way I'd look forward to a date with someone I really like?

Part of what made me shy was I had a severe lisp. People several times told me after we got to know each other that when they had first met me, they assumed I was stupid because of my lisp.

HOW TO MAKE YOUR FAMILY BUSINESS LAST

Over the years, knowing that some people initially felt this way about me magnified my innate shyness. There's also the fact that my first marriage was as unhappy as my real marriage to Frank was happy. Translation: my first marriage was bitterly, miserably unhappy. It eroded my self-confidence.

I didn't want to have a phobia of speaking, and when one day a woman from the Business and Professional Women's Clubs called (it was a cold call), asking if I'd like to take their public speaking and self-confidence course, I signed up.

It had a huge impact. I learned not to fear public speaking. In fact, I enjoyed what I was learning so much that at the end of the Business and Professional Women's Club course, I joined them to become a life member, and then signed up for the Dale Carnegie public speaking course.

That was the beginning of probably a dozen public speaking courses and reading many dozens of books on public speaking. I also spent an entire year, beginning at age 38, with a speech therapist learning to overcome my lisp.

At the end of that year of self-development, I was invited to be a guest on KXTV in Sacramento. After the show finished, the station manager said I was a natural for television and gave me my own TV interview show.

With some training and an attitude change, I went from someone too shy to use the telephone to someone who ended up with a syndicated TV show.

It wasn't that I had all that much talent, but I did have a grounding in the basics, and that was enough. I still think that if I could do it, most anyone could.

Well, dear friend, back to you. Can you become a communicator?

The answer is yes, in the same way that if you practice, and there's no physical impediment, you can learn to play tennis. You need to know the fundamentals, and that means lessons and classes, and lots of practice.

I think it's worth it. The dividends in self-confidence and ability to influence are completely life-changing. In my case, they enabled me to escape a toxic marriage and helped me be ready for a blissful one.

Checklist for Developing Communications Skills

In my life, I've observed that some people are naturals at writing and speaking. For the rest of us, these are skills that take study and practice.

> **Read books**

> **Take courses**

> **Join organizations like Toastmasters**

> **Practice every chance you can get.**

> **If you want to be professional about it, take the year-long Speakers' Academy at your local National Speakers Association.**

Resources:

How to Write Magazine Articles that Sell, W.P. Williams, 1979. This is available through 3rd party sellers on Amazon. It's an old book, but by using the techniques in it, I ended up as a syndicated columnist. It's a powerful book.

Public speaking courses: http://www.dalecarnegie.com My father, my husband, and I all took the Dale Carnegie public speaking course. And Frank got so much out of it that he sent many of the members of his top management to take the course as well.

https://www.toastmasters.org has a great record for developing speakers skills.

The National Speakers Association can help equip you to take your speaking to a professional level. To find a Speakers' Academy near you, go to: http://www.nsaspeaker.org/chapter-leadership/chapters-speakers-academy/

CHAPTER 35

FACING A MEDIA INTERVIEW? FEAR FEELS WORSE THAN IT LOOKS

The odds are, sometime in your life you're going to find yourself with a microphone in front of you, and you'll be on the air. It could happen voluntarily: maybe you want to promote your product or a charity or a cause.

Maybe it will happen by accident: you're part of a person in the street interview, or who knows, you could be the hero in a hijacking attempt.

One way or the other, it's worth knowing how to do your best when you're confronted with such a situation. As part of a family business, you are a walking embodiment of the brand and it helps everyone if you perform well.

The tip I'm about to share with you is the same one that I've given the more than 2,500 guests I had on my syndicated television show, *Country Magazine*. I no longer have the show–I gave it up when I married Frank, but the tip still works and I still give talks on what you're about to read.

About 90% of my guests on *Country Magazine* had never been on TV before. However, with the tips I give them before we'd go on the air, I've never had one who couldn't find the right words or looked scared.

And by the way, I usually had only 15 minutes in the Green Room to help my guests feel comfortable before we were on the air. Frequently, when I first met them at the TV station, they were nervous and miserable.

They usually had something they wanted to say, but I knew that if I couldn't get them to feel relaxed and if I couldn't get them to enjoy experience, they might forget what they were saying or even freeze. If they didn't do well, I wouldn't do well.

For many reasons, I was highly motivated to learn how to make my guests feel comfortable and at ease. If I were with you right now, and if you were about to go on the air, this is the kind of information I'd share with you. You'd discover that it works!

Attitude and Self-Confidence

The magic key to coming across well is self-confidence. When you're confident, the words flow, your posture will be good, and you'll enjoy the experience.

So how do we get self-confidence? The first tip for helping you with self-confidence is knowing that fear feels worse than it looks.

You may have heard the expression, "The camera never lies." Broadcasters even joke about this when they, say, "Physicians bury their mistakes, and architects cover them with ivy. But when you're on the air, your mistakes are right out there for everyone to see."

That kind of thinking is enough to make anyone nervous. But not to worry. The fact is, the camera does lie. Every day. No matter how terrified you're feeling inside, the camera is almost certainly not going to show it, and you're going to look just fine.

HOW TO MAKE YOUR FAMILY BUSINESS LAST

Relax, the Camera Does Lie

Television has an odd characteristic of filtering out strong feeling. To have people know that you're terrified would take considerable acting ability on your part. Television actors know that they must magnify and exaggerate emotions to have those emotions recognizable on TV.

I know this firsthand. I once taped a show on honey bees, with a swarm of 50,000 bees on my hand-held mike. Normally bees don't scare me, but this case was different.

I was interviewing Norman Gary, a professor of bee biology from the University of California at. Davis. We were in an almond orchard, and for dramatic effect, he had put a chemical (technically a pheromone) on my mike that orders the bees that were in the orchard, to come to Mitzi, *now!*

The drama part of this was the camera could catch the ever-growing number of bees on my mike as we talked.   This was fine with me, except something went wrong with the TV camera and we had to do the interview twice.

Have you ever tried to hold your arm out for 10 minutes with no rest? Now, suddenly I find myself having to do this for close to 20 minutes as we re-did the segment.

 By the time of the second taping, the bees formed a mass the size of a basketball. Even worse, there were ever more bees coming every second.

The more bees that came to my mike, the more they were chemically signaling to their sisters, "Hey, come here! Mitzi's microphone is where the action is!"

HOW TO MAKE YOUR FAMILY BUSINESS LAST

My arm muscles were getting so exhausted it felt as if they were turning to water. This, dear friends, is a problem because the entire point of this show was telling everyone how to avoid getting stung.

Staying very still when you're around bees is the entire secret.

Ooops! I was doing the exact opposite!

I could feel my muscles starting to shake—in other words the very last thing I wanted when I have roughly 500 times more bees on my body than it would take to kill me.

More bees still kept coming, and my arm was getting weaker by the millisecond. I was scared for my life.

In my mind I was having visions of my beloved sons growing up without their mother. Moment by moment this seemed ever more likely. I was thinking how much I loved them and I was trying to will myself to keep my arm still…but I couldn't, and I was as thoroughly terrified as I've ever been in my life.

It turned out OK and I lived to tell the tale, Dr. Gary rescued me by blowing smoke at the bees, making them confused and unable to sting. I survived, but it was the scariest time of my life.

And now for the surprising thing and the reason I'm sharing this story with you: when the show aired later, people raved over my supposed fearlessness.
 Even I who knew that I was scared for my life couldn't see the existential terror that I knew was there. The camera simply filtered out the emotions.

HOW TO MAKE YOUR FAMILY BUSINESS LAST

I saw the same thing recently when I watched a man accused of embezzlement being deposed for a million-dollar lawsuit. The deposition was videotaped, and I could either watch him in person, or I could turn slightly and watch how he looked on the TV monitor.

When I switched back and forth between reality and the screen, I could barely believe I was watching the same event – even though it was happening right there in front of me.

In person, the man looked so nervous that it hurt to be in the same room with him. He looked pale and haunted. On the screen, he looked composed, reasonable, and in control. The camera's filtering effect erased the fear that was so obvious in person.

With luck, you'll never be in a situation that stressful, but remember, the camera does lie. You will almost certainly come across more much more poised and self-confident than you really feel.

Just as fear feeds on itself, so self-confidence feeds on itself; when you know you're looking self-confident, you can actually be self-confident. You will almost certainly come across as more self-confident than you really feel. Fear feels worse than it looks.

Checklist for Self-Confidence

> **Think about how you're almost certainly going to look more confident than you feel.**
> This will be the case as the camera isn't good at showing normal, garden-variety fear. You're going to look just fine.

Once you know that the fear isn't showing, you can relax and actually feel more confident.

CHAPTER 36

THE BEST MEDIA TIP: TALK AS IF YOU'RE SPEAKING TO A FRIEND

The best media tip I know is an attitude tip: when you're on television, you're never addressing millions of people at once. Millions may be watching, but keep in mind that you're talking to individuals, usually only one or two people at a time in their homes; it's never as if you're talking to a crowd in a stadium.

When I was first on TV, I would have been paralyzed and probably couldn't have gotten a word out if I had considered the number of people watching. On top of that, I had a genuine phobia of public speaking.

Being on Television: A Recipe for Terror

There are studies that say that glossophobia (fear of public speaking) is the greatest fear that Americans have, even greater than spiders or death itself. When it came to glossophobia, I was right up there with the best of them.

Anyway, the tip about imagining you're talking with one or two people at a time saved me. What happened was, I was a guest on a local farm show, and as a rice grower (which I was back then) I was highly motivated to get people on my side on an issue that was before the legislature.

It was economically a life and death issue; if the legislation had gone the wrong way for us, I along with much of the rice industry could have been put out of business.

As I said, I was scared enough of public speaking that without the tip that television is an intimate medium and you're not talking with a whole stadium, I doubt if I could have put two sentences together.

However, I imagined that I was talking with one of my best friends from California Women for Agriculture. She was an older woman, and I imagined her kindly face, nodding, and interested.

Imagination, a Friend, and the Fear That Vanished

In the CBS studio in Sacramento where this took place, when the little red tally light lit up, indicating that the broadcast was live, I looked deep into the camera, as if the lens were a window into my friend's living room. I imagined I was talking with my friend about something I knew would interest her.

With this attitude, I found that I was enjoying the experience. I not only felt upbeat and happy, I felt that I was at my best. After all, I was talking with someone I liked and I knew I had something important to offer her.

Today, whenever I'm on the air, whether it's radio or television, I always have the attitude that I'm communicating with one person, someone I like, someone I'm eager to share things with.

The result is, I feel as comfortable as I would be talking in my own living room.

Think about this for a moment. Whatever it is that you'd be talking about – your work, your charity, your team, the family business–wouldn't you feel comfortable talking about it with a couple of people in their homes?

In fact, if you like your subject, wouldn't you enjoy the chance to discuss the things you really care about? That's the mental attitude to strive for when you're on the air.

It will do wonders for your self-confidence. You'll feel much more relaxed and comfortable, and you'll do a better job. And this counts because you're representing not just yourself but also, as a member of a family business, how people see you may influence how they see the brand.

Checklist for Being Comfortable on TV

TV is an intimate medium.
Imagine you're speaking to one or two people in their living rooms rather than millions.

Remember that you have important and useful information to share.
This isn't about you, it's about what you can do for them. When you're thinking about what you're doing to benefit your audience, there's less mind space available for worrying about yourself.

Imagine speaking with friends.
These are people who want to hear what you're saying.

CHAPTER 37

PREPARING FOR A MEDIA INTERVIEW: MAKE IT EASY ON YOURSELF

If you know you're going to be interviewed, put some time into preparing. It's worth putting effort into preparing because as a family member, people may view you as representing the family business as well as yourself.

Preparation is so important to self-confidence that Dale Carnegie once said, "One great lesson stands out like Mount Everest, towering above all the others: only the prepared speaker deserves to be confident."

The first part of your preparation is finding out what kind of show you'll be on. Is it a news show or an interview show? Will you be on for sixty seconds or half an hour? Is it live or taped? Is your host friendly or hostile?

Length of Time You're On

If it's 60 seconds during a news show, figure out how to make your point as concisely as possible. If you can, plan a vivid, quotable phrase that encapsulates your point.

If, on the other hand, it's an interview show where you'll be on for five minutes or more, you don't have to worry so much about giving short, concise answers. As a TV hostess, I loved enthusiastic guests who have a lot to say, and longer answers made my job easier.

Live or Taped

If your part is taped for insertion into a later broadcast, plan

209

to make your point first, and explain it afterwards. This is a precaution in case the editor cuts off part of what you say. The editor will have a hard time editing out the beginning of your talk, but it's relatively easy to cut off the end.

News or Interview

If it's a news show, you'll be lucky if you're on for 30 seconds. You may have no time at all to prepare, except for what you already know. But if you've read through the self-confidence tips in previous chapters, you will do a good job.

If it's an interview show, you'll probably have several weeks to prepare. If you follow the next few steps, your performance will be better than 90% of the talk show guests, and you'll have a good chance of being invited back.

First, know your facts. As with public speaking, don't even try to talk about any subject unless you know a great deal more about it than your audience.

If you're not confident that you already know that much, then prepare for your interview the same way you prepare for a speech: know at least ten times more about your subject than your audience does.

When I'm facing a radio or television interview, even when it's on a topic I know well, I spend a couple of hours collecting the most current facts and figures. I make a list of this information so I can review it and have it fresh in my mind just before I go on the air.

HOW TO MAKE YOUR FAMILY BUSINESS LAST

Bring a Prop

Next, plan an attention-getting prop or props to illustrate what you're saying. Props are, if possible, even more important on television than they are in platform speaking; they take you out of the category of being a "talking head."

You don't want to be a "talking head" because, with only a few rare exceptions, (gifted politicians are an example of an exception), talking heads don't hold people's attention. Producers hate talking heads for just that reason.

If you bring in some exciting prop, your host or hostess will appreciate it. In addition, you'll discover that this atmosphere will do wonders for your confidence level.

A fringe benefit of having a prop, is it immediately solves one of the problems most beginners face, and that's what to do with your hands. If you have a prop in your hands, you've got something to do with them.

When I'm giving "how to" talks on television appearances, I love to challenge my audiences to see if anyone has a topic that can't be illustrated. By now I don't believe there is any such animal.

One way or another, anything can be shown as well as discussed. Use your imagination. In fact, now's a good time to brain storm and figure out five ways you could illustrate what you're going to say. Some of the possibilities are charts, slides, photographs, demonstrations, videos, a live animal, or a product.

HOW TO MAKE YOUR FAMILY BUSINESS LAST

Possible Props
1._____
2._____
3._____
4._____
5._____

From the point of view of a TV program, the best prop is something that reinforces your point, that moves, and that involves action on your part. It's wonderful if it's something people have never seen before.

If you really want to hold people's attention, surveys show that sex, violence, and humor work best.

If we could meet in person, I'd try to suggest props that could illustrate your message, whatever it is. To take some examples:

- If you're talking about seeing-eye dogs, bring one in and show the dog guiding a blind person through an obstacle course that you've set up in the studio.

- If you're talking about self-defense, show how you'd mug your interviewer- and what he or she could do in defense.

- If you're talking about the need for calcium in the diet, bring in a skeleton with deteriorated calcium-poor bones, and maybe even brutally crush one of those porous bones with your fingers.

Checklist for Preparation

Be sure to budget time for preparation.
You need this for your best performance, so why not give yourself your best shot at doing well?

Find out about the show.
News? Interview? Length of time you're on? Live or taped?

Don't be a talking head.
Whatever it is you're talking about, bring a prop that illustrates it, or show a video or a slide of it, or use a chart to show what's happening to it.

Practice your demonstration.
If you're demonstrating with your prop, practice the demonstration from start to finish at least fifteen times until you're over-prepared.

Have a Plan B in case the prop or demonstration doesn't go as planned.
In my TV career, I've witnessed many dozens of demonstrations that didn't go the way they were supposed to. You don't want that to happen, but still, it could. Figure out what you'd do.

CHAPTER 38

A MEDIA INTERVIEW: HOW YOU SOUND AND HOW YOU LOOK

Since you've chosen to read this section, I'm going to assume there's a good chance that a media interview may be in the cards for you. If so, I'd like to give you every chance to sound and look your best.

Here are some tips that professionals use to improve how they sound and look:

Practice Using a Video or Audio Recorder

Professional spokespeople frequently practice answering questions using a video recorder. Get a friend to ask you likely questions. Then analyze your answers and see if you can improve.

Use this checklist as a guide.

- Is my posture erect and confident?

- Am I enthusiastic and energetic?

- Do I use appropriate gestures? (You don't want to look like a stick.)

- Are my answers focused, with a point and supporting material?

- Am I friendly?

One important thing is something not to do. Don't memorize answers; just as with public speaking, canned answers tend not to hold people's attention. My theory is, the deeper it comes from you, the deeper it will reach your audience.

Develop Fluency around a Microphone

If you have trouble speaking easily around a microphone, try the "Jim Johnson technique." Jim worked for the U.S. Department of Agriculture, and he was one of my favorite broadcasters when I was in the business.

When he was first starting as a broadcaster, he'd take a tape recorder, look at a wall in his office, and then try to describe everything on it. At first, he could only talk for a matter of seconds before he'd get tongue-tied and run out of things to say.

Later, he told me, he could look at a nearly empty wall and talk for an hour if necessary. Practicing meant he developed perfect fluency.

By the way, I'm not suggesting hour-long answers. The point of Jim Johnson's exercise is to develop a fluency in thinking and talking when there's a microphone around.

Appearance and Self-Confidence

Here are some appearance factors that should help your self-confidence. By the way, appearance does count. I remember when I was first starting out, I asked an old timer at KXTV how important appearance is.

He answered, "Don't worry about it at all, Mitzi, just don't worry about it—unless you want to make a good impression!"

HOW TO MAKE YOUR FAMILY BUSINESS LAST

Checklist for looking good on TV

> **Use good posture.** If you keep your back straight rather than slumped, you'll look more authoritative, more believable, and more energetic.
>
> **Keep your legs either together or crossed.** If you'd been in the control rooms that I've been in and heard the whoops of laughter every time the cameras caught a guest in a "crotch shot," you would never – but never – let anyone catch you that way.
>
> **Wear clothes that photograph well.** Your all-time best bet is some shade of blue. This is the most flattering to all skin tones, regardless of race. Most colors will work quite well, except fire-engine red, which is risky because it can make some skin colors look sallow on camera.
>
> **Avoid large areas of either black or white.** Black clothing can look like a black hole on screen, and you're safer avoiding large areas of white because white can glare and it can also make the areas around it look washed out.
>
> **Avoid shiny distractions.** Narrow stripes or chevrons are also an unfortunate choice because on some of the older screens, they'll give an appearance of shimmering. Large jewelry pieces that will glint or patent shoes that will glimmer will distract people from your message. I've had people say, "I think it would be just great to have something to distract the viewers from me." My answer is, "As long as you've got precious television time – and it can be worth anywhere from

216

hundreds of dollars to hundreds of thousands of dollars a minute –you want to give yourself the best chance of getting your message across. You don't want anything to distract your audience from your message."

For men's makeup, use powder! Remember that overhead lights emphasize any shininess, especially if you're balding. It's frequently hot in the studio with all those lights, so if you have any tendency to perspire, give yourself a little powdering. If you're at one of the larger studios, they'll have a makeup artist do this for you.

For women's makeup, wear what makes you feel comfortable. This is the most important rule. If you never wear makeup, and you're going to feel all weird wearing it now, then skip it. Many of my guests have chosen to do just that, and I think they made the right choice. But having said that, let me add that television washes out colors, and you'll look abnormally pale with no makeup. If you're on the fence about whether to wear it or not, *wear it!*

For women's makeup part 2, wear more than you think you need. If you are comfortable with it, (and I hope you are or can talk yourself into it) wear as much make-up as you'd wear in the evening to the dressiest dance – and then a tad more.

I remember being shocked my first few months as a TV hostess because my colleagues urged me to put on so much makeup that I thought I looked not just like a professional, but like a member of the Oldest Profession. But when I'd see the results on the videotapes later, I had to admit that the overdone makeup looked normal on screen.

If you're at a large studio, they'll have a makeup artist available to make the decision for you. (Oh, and as a quick aside, talk with the makeup artist! They're one of the best sources of really interesting stories about famous people, whether politicians or authors or famous actors or actresses. Having your make up done at a TV studio can be a fun time, and I think part of their job is to help you feel relaxed by telling really neat stories. But they'll also leave you alone if you need to focus your thoughts.)

CHAPTER 39

ANXIOUS ABOUT MAKING A MISTAKE IN AN INTERVIEW? NOT TO WORRY!

One of the big factors that can undermine your self-confidence on radio or television or public speaking in general is fear of making a mistake. However, I have some amazingly good news for you. And you don't have to take my word for it: I'm going to prove it to you.

The good news is, most people won't notice your mistake. Or at least they won't, if you'll follow this one tip that professionals know and amateurs don't.

When You Make a Mistake, Glide Right On By

If you don't draw attention to a mistake, almost no one will notice it. To you, a mispronounced name or a stutter or some other flub will stand out more than all the glittering lights on Broadway.

To your audience, your fluff won't even penetrate their consciousness. That is, unless you point it out in some way which unfortunately, unless you've been coached, you almost certainly will.

The un-coached person has an almost irresistible urge to apologize or roll his or her eyes heavenward, or simply act very embarrassed. If instead of drawing attention to your mistake, you either glide right on by it, or unobtrusively correct it, chances are, only a media professional will notice.

HOW TO MAKE YOUR FAMILY BUSINESS LAST

To prove this to yourself, listen to network broadcasters, but instead of concentrating on what they're saying, look for flubs. Once you're focusing on mistakes, you'll be stunned by how many mistakes even the top anchors make.

Almost no one, even the top professionals, gets through a single broadcast without some kind of flub. We normally don't notice the mistakes, though, because that's not where we're focusing our attention.

I like to demonstrate this principal to audiences by asking the members to close their eyes and then I ask them if they know the color and pattern of the carpet in the room we're all in. When I tell them to open their eyes and they see, for example, a fuchsia rug with gold squares woven into it, they're astonished that they never noticed it, even though it was right there for everyone to see.

Unless an individual recently bought a carpet, or is a decorator, or maybe has heard me speak before, I can count on him or her not having noticed the carpet. That's not where anyone's focus of attention was.

The mistakes you make on the air are a little like the carpet in the background. Unless you get flustered and draw attention to mistakes, the odds are that no one will notice, much less remember.

In fact, one of the big differences between a professional broadcaster and a person who hasn't been coached is that the professional will just continue after a mistake, never drawing attention to it; nonprofessionals may become so flustered over an error that they immediately make three more.

So, don't worry if you fluff something. If you don't draw attention to it, you may be the only one who notices.

Serious Mistakes Can Even Be an Advantage

But let's suppose your nightmare has come true: you've made a great, big, highly-visible mistake. Imagine for a long, terrible moment that you don't just stumble over a line or get a name wrong. Instead, you really flub it. You forget your train of thought or just can't think of what to say.

Even so, all is not lost. In my experience on TV, the guests who got the most fan mail were not the slick and practiced professionals. No, it was the genuine human beings who made mistakes and were just like other normal human beings.

I don't know what my boss at KXTV would have said if he had known this, but I stopped worrying even a little bit when I blew something, and it's not because I didn't care.

I cared very much, but I didn't worry because I knew that I would get twice as much fan mail. I believe the reason is that viewers relate much more to someone human than to someone perfect.

People Relate to People Who Are Human, Not to People Who Are Perfect

My favorite example of this was a tomato grower I was interviewing in his tomato field. He was explaining how his van-size tomato harvester worked, and then…horror!...he forgot what he was saying.

HOW TO MAKE YOUR FAMILY BUSINESS LAST

That was my first year in my job, and if I had had more experience, I would have sensed his problem and jumped in and verbally rescued him before anyone noticed. But back then....ugh! It happened.

His mistake was something everyone would notice, and he knew it. He told me that after the show was over, he went behind one of his packing sheds and spent four hours shoveling dirt from one pile to another and then back again.

He was trying to deal with his embarrassment and humiliation. His dark mood persisted for several days until.....wait for it! ....until the fan letters began pouring in! People loved him!

They related to him!

Older ladies wanted to mother him.

Younger ladies proposed marriage.

Men thought he was great and would like to be friends.

The TV audience had absolutely adored seeing a real person who was "one of us."

By contrast, the most perfect, most professional guest I ever had got an entirely different reception. She was a pineapple queen, from Hawaii.

She was so beautiful and graceful that the female members of the camera crew and I agreed that if there's reincarnation, we wanted to come back as her. She was as close to perfection in every aspect of her manner and appearance as you could get in this world.

HOW TO MAKE YOUR FAMILY BUSINESS LAST

In addition, she delivered her lines in honeyed tones that were so beautiful you could almost, as Steve Jobs once said, "lick them." Her demonstrations went beautifully, she hit her marks exactly, her timing was perfection.

She didn't get even one fan letter after the show. She reinforces my view that audiences are much more likely to like you for being human than for being perfect.

And that brings me back again to the thought that serious mistakes aren't necessarily too serious. To repeat, people are more likely to like you for showing that you're human.

Checklist for Dealing with Mistake on Camera

> **It's normal to fluff a date or get something else wrong.** Almost no professional broadcaster can get through a broadcast without making a mistake. Don't beat yourself up over it.

> **If (or better, when) you make a mistake, glide right on by.** If it's important to correct it, do so without drawing attention to it. The odds are that nobody but you will be aware of your fluff.

> **If it's a Big Serious mistake, this may very well be an advantage.** Audiences relate to people who are human much more than they relate to people who are perfect.

CHAPTER 40

DEALING WITH A HOSTILE INTERVIEWER: SAFETY NET PHRASES CAN HELP YOU

If you know you're facing a media interview, either listen to the show ahead of time or find out from others what kind of interviewer you're up against.

I was always a friendly interviewer, and I viewed my job as giving my guest his or her best shot at telling his or her story. Friendly interviewers want you to look good, and we'll use all the tricks we know to make you feel relaxed, comfortable, and at your best.

There Are Interviewers Who Want You to Squirm

But I have colleagues who believe that the more their guests squirm, the higher their own ratings will be.

Now don't get me wrong. Ratings aren't everything to TV people. Oxygen, for example, is more important.

A hostile interviewer looking for ratings can be highly motivated to make you just as uncomfortable as he or she can. What can you do?

Lots!

Safety Net Phrases

Having been on the receiving end of many hundreds of interviews, both as an author and as a former president of

HOW TO MAKE YOUR FAMILY BUSINESS LAST

American Agri-Women, I've found that having "safety net" phrases can get me through just about anything.

The advantage of having safety net phrases prepared ahead of time is, they give you time to think. It's best to develop your own, but in a moment, I'll share some that have worked so well for me that I no longer worry about even the most vicious interviewer.

To get the maximum benefit from the safety net phrases, make a list of the questions you'd most hate being asked. Then get a friend to ask you the hostile questions.

Now answer the questions you don't want to be asked, prefacing your answer with a safety net phrase. When you master this technique, hostile interviewers will have a harder time catching you off balance.

Here's a sampling of ones that have worked for me, but before you read them, please keep in mind that your safety net phrases will only work for you if they reflect you, your beliefs, and your situation. *In other words, don't copy mine,* unless by miracle they just happen to fit you. In the examples, I use agriculture, but substitute your subject to make it appropriate for you.

Checklist of Safety Net Phrases

> **Baiting–type questions** One response might be, "I understand your concern because I used to feel that way myself, until I found out that...." and then continue with a couple of good facts that support your view. This sympathetic approach can turn a confrontational atmosphere into a friendlier one. But don't use this unless you sincerely mean it.

Global questions that you don't feel qualified to answer Try substituting your own area of expertise for references to agriculture: "I can't speak for all of agriculture, but I can tell you that on my farm…" and then relate the global question to how it affects your experience. You are an expert on that, and audiences will find personal experiences a hundred times more engaging than abstract opinions.

Questions that you don't know the answer to You can always say, "I don't know." That's legitimate, but you could make your answer more humorous by saying, "I'll give you a straight answer to that, and you'll be glad to hear that there is no one listening to us today who will contradict me: the answer is, "I don't know!" That usually gets a friendly laugh, and I've discovered that it's hard for interviewers to be really hostile to you if they've just laughed with you.

Questions with many parts Don't feel that you must answer them all. Just pick out the one part that you're most comfortable with and answer that. Make sure that you consciously determine to answer the one that you'll do best with. I don't know why it is, but somehow, we can be almost irresistibly drawn to answer the part that is most threatening. Interviewers count on this – so don't get sucked in. After taking a split second to decide what part of the question will help you most, you might say, "You just mentioned _____, and in my experience…." Now you're off and running. I've almost never had an interviewer circle back and ask the other parts of the question, since my answer usually leads them off on some different tack.

Questions based on misinformation By all means correct the question, but do it tactfully. For example, "I think a lot of people in my industry would be more comfortable if the question were worded...." and then rephrase the question, using correct information. Be aware, though, that it's a tricky thing to correct a host on the air; use all the tact you can muster because you don't want to make him or her look bad. If you embarrass the host, the viewers will tend to rally around him and resent you. After all, most tuned in because they know and like the host, not because they know and like you.

Questions that start with "I know for a fact..." Don't comment on it or agree with it unless you know that it is a fact. Answer instead, "I haven't seen that research," "or "I haven't seen the article you're referring to." This way you avoid authenticating a "fact" that may not be a fact.

"What if" questions? These questions can get people into lots of trouble. Public relations experts just about unanimously suggest that we avoid answering them. One of the best ways of handling one is simply not answering it and instead saying, "Instead of taking a hypothetical case, let's talk about _____." And then you bridge onto something you do want to talk about. You could say, "You know, I really think your audience would be interested to know that..." and quickly stick in the points that you'd like to get across.

Memorize and practice your own personal, suited-to-you "safety net" phrases that you're likely to need.

By the way, I generally don't recommend memorizing answers because they could sound robotic. "Safety net" phrases are an exception because when they're at the tip of your tongue, they can come across as being quite natural.

Just having them available can help your self-confidence and can get you through an interview that might otherwise be traumatic.

CHAPTER 41

WRITING FOR YOUR FAMILY: KEEP YOUR GOAL IN MIND

We've been talking about communication involving the public, but what about writing for your own family?

If you are writing for a literary magazine or a creative writing course, be as artistic and original as you choose. But for communicating with the family, the goal is to be clear and accessible.

An Easy and Reasonable Goal

Unless you've had a lot of practice in writing, a reasonable goal is to be so clear that people focus on the content of what you're saying and pay little attention to how you're saying it. You don't have to be fancy.

Checklist for Readable Writing

Use tools for proofreading and readability. Microsoft Word has some great proofreading tools that also measure your readability. YouTube has some good videos showing how to access these tools for proofreading and readability.

Aim for sentences no longer than 20 words. There are exceptions of course, but as a general rule, shorter sentences are easier to follow than longer ones.

Have variety in sentence length.
Some sentences could be five words and some 20 words.

Have sentences that you can read using just one breath.

Use shorter words.
If you have a choice between a shorter word or a longer one, generally choose the shorter one.

Avoid words or phrases in foreign languages.
Some of your audience may know these words, but others may not.

Use shorter paragraphs.
Often two sentences per paragraph is a good choice. College-educated people will easily handle longer paragraphs, but your family may not all have graduated from college, and your goal is to have your writing feel welcoming and accessible to all family members.

Good writing includes both facts and stories.
Our minds are wired to remember stories so it's good to use them. But facts are worthwhile also because facts strengthen and anchor the stories.

Support statements with evidence.

Organize the material so it has a logical flow.

If possible, use graphic design elements to make your points.
Headings, white space, and bullets can be used to emphasize and highlight important ideas.

References:

Here are three references that I like:

The Elements of Style: Updated and Annotated for Present-Day Use 2nd Edition
by Mr. Stanford K. Pritchard (Author). This is a 2012 version of the book many of us studied in high school.

The Sense of Style: The Thinking Person's Guide to Writing in the 21st Century, 2014
by Steven Pinker (Author)

The Art of Styling Sentences: 20 Patterns for Success (Paperback) by Marie L. Waddell, et al. This is a 1993 book, and it's a favorite.

CHAPTER 42

HOW TO WRITE ALMOST ANYTHING: TRICKS OF THE TRADE

If you want influence, prestige, and if you'd like to be perceived as an authority, here's a shortcut. Write articles, books, or blogs.

The advantages of being a published writer are huge. The visibility that comes with it will not only impact your career and your brand, the research you'll do in order to be expert enough to be published will force you to grow as a person.

Still, writing is not easy or everyone would do it. A publisher once told my father that 10,000 people think about writing a book for every person who writes one.

Who knows how accurate that statement is, but my goal is for you to be the one who does it instead of thinks about it. Here's the technique that's helped me write more than 1800 published articles.

What you're about to read assumes you've already done the necessary research. We're talking here about the actual process of putting words on paper, words that others will eventually read.

Writing, in Five Drafts

Listed below are suggestions for how to outline your drafts:

HOW TO MAKE YOUR FAMILY BUSINESS LAST

First Draft:

During the first draft, your goal is quantity, not quality. Pick the number of words you'll aim for each day, whether it's 300 words or 3000 and just churn them out.

Be aware that some days, your product will be horrible, but at this stage, that doesn't matter. The principle that we're after here is, your very rough draft is like brainstorming: it will spark something better during later drafts.

Meanwhile, just keep spouting out stuff even if it feels unbelievably awful. This is not the time to be critical; it's the time to be productive. For me, this stage is the longest, takes the most effort, and is the least pleasant.

Now, the most important part of this stage is, don't allow yourself to do any polishing or re-writing until you've finished the entire article, blog, or book. In other words, you have a complete draft, page one to the end before you do any fine-tuning or polishing.

I have three reasons for this, and collectively, they're so strong that I now never allow exceptions to the rule about no polishing or re-writing until the first draft is done:

- The mental state that's needed for putting thoughts into words needs to be creativity, not criticality. You want the ideas to come out, whether they're good or bad. You can improve on them later, but now you're laying a foundation. My principle is, "It's easy to improve on something but difficult to improve on nothing." The first draft is about putting something on paper that you can improve later.

- The act of polishing is not only a different mindset, it's also too easy to spend time polishing and never finishing.

- When you finish your first draft, you may find that you can't use parts that you put a lot of effort into polishing. It's painful to cut things that you've already polished, so don't polish to begin with.

But what if you must stop and look up a name or date or some background material?

Guess what!

I don't.

I use a made-up "place holder name" or date or whatever, and I write it in bolded capitals with a note CORRECT THIS LATER. For the first draft it's against the rules to slow down the creative "gush" to do research.

I also keep a file folder "Act on later," where I write notes on what I need to address later.

Second Draft:

For the 2nd draft, go through your entire draft and make any big structural changes that you need such as reordering the chapters or cutting parts that don't fit.

Third Draft

For the 3rd draft, go through your entire draft and fill in any missing information. By the end of the 3rd draft, you'll have a complete article or book or blog with 99% of the information there. The writing is unpolished and may suck, but rejoice because you are now in a wonderful position for the next stage.

Fourth Draft

Yay! You're now at the most fun part, the fourth draft. Here's where you try for your best writing.

- Do the sentences flow from one to the next?

- Are they easy to understand, or might someone have to re-read it to get it?

- Is there a variety of sentence length?

- What about variety in sentence structure?

- Can you come up with better metaphors and similes?

- Have you used the exact word for what you're trying to express?

- Is there any chance to sneak in some humor, or maybe add the perfect story to illustrate your point?

When you've finished the fourth draft you're ready to show it to your friends and critics. Ask them to let you know when something isn't clear, or if you've repeated yourself, or they just don't like a passage.

Also, ask them if unintentionally you've said something offensive or that could be taken the wrong way. It happens!

Beg them to be as honest as they can because you need feedback. Almost no one can judge his or her own writing, and your honest critic is your friend.

Fifth Draft

Woohoo, you're at your fifth and final draft. Here you incorporate the changes recommended by your friends, to the extent that they make sense to you. Give it one last polish, and you're ready for the printers or publishers.
While you're doing all this, keep in mind something that the late Nido Quebein, famous inspirational public speaker used to say. "If you really want to do something, you'll find a way. If you don't, then you'll find an excuse."
Translation: don't find excuses! This is something you want to do, right?

Checklist for Writing Anything

Influence, Prestige and Authority!
Remember, writing articles, blogs, or books is a shortcut to influence, prestige, and authority. Do it!

Use the Five stages:

- o First Draft: For this stage, just put the words on paper, expecting that the product isn't going to be great.

- o Second Draft: Make any structural changes you need to such as changing the order of the chapters or the arguments.

- o Third Draft: Fill in any missing information such as names or dates or titles. When you've finished the third draft, you've got a document that begins on page one and continues to the end with no missing information.

- o Fourth Draft: This is the fun part. Polish, rewrite, and use your best skills for making it flow smoothly, be easy to understand and fun to read. When you've finished your fourth draft, you're ready to show it to friends or experts.

- o Fifth Draft: You incorporate the changes that others have recommended and that make sense to you. At the end of this, you're ready to send it out for publication.

Resource:

Writing that Works: How to Communicate Effectively in Business, 3rd Edition, Kenneth Roman and Joel Raphaelson,

CONCLUSION

I'm going to confess to you why I wrote this book. My purpose in life is to increase happiness and decrease misery. While bringing about world peace would accomplish that goal quite nicely, thank you, to the best of my knowledge, that job isn't an offer!

So, what I found I could do is use my background and experience to be a part of solving one of the biggest pain points for family businesses. Building a family business takes almost unbelievable commitment and sacrifice, and seeing it all go poof if the family splits apart can be agony.

I'm haunted by a recent conversation with an 80-year old man who was suicidal. A family quarrel had destroyed his company. His life had lost most of its meaning now that his legacy had vanished and his children wouldn't speak to him or to each other.

There are situations that are more painful, but having your life's work destroyed by a family quarrel ranks high up on the human pain scale. If only the man I just mentioned had known early on about some of the resources that could have helped prevent this family tragedy.

Alas, his experience isn't unique. I know of case after case where a disintegrating family meant a disintegrating business. The collateral damage to everyone and to everything the business touched was devastating. The pain this causes the family can last for generations.

The good news is, it doesn't need to be this way. Family businesses can teach their members how to have a chance at being supportive and loving. But this information rarely comes about by accident.

HOW TO MAKE YOUR FAMILY BUSINESS LAST

Family members need to know that: they're part of something bigger than themselves; that they can't always get their way; that they're stewards of a family legacy; that they'll occasionally need to sacrifice for the good of the whole; and that values trump material things.

So, whatever your age, take action now to help your family business last. Don't leave things to chance. Use the tools in this book, including the sections on:

- Ways of building a strong and positive family culture

- Tools for dealing with the inevitable problems that can affect any family businesses

- Advice for soft skills that can build the family's talent stack, making the family more effective and more resilient

Dear friends, so far the communication between us has been a monologue. I'd love it if you'd turn it into a dialogue. Tell me about what's working and what's not. My e-mail is Mitzi@MitziPerdue.com and I'd love to hear from you.

Oh, one more thing: if your organization is looking for a professional public speaker, please keep me in mind.

My website is: www.MitziPerdue.com

ABOUT THE AUTHOR

Mitzi Perdue holds a BA with honors degree from Harvard University and an MPA from the George Washington University. She is a past president of the 35,000 American Agri-Women, a former syndicated columnist for Scripps Howard, and her television series, Country Magazine was syndicated to 76 stations. She's the founder of CERES Farms, the family-owned agricultural real estate investment company that has owned rice fields, commercial and residential real estate, and today, the family vineyards sell wine grapes to well-known wineries such as Mondavi, Bogle, Folie a Deux, and Toasted Head.

As an author and public speaker, Mitzi specializes in sharing the tools, techniques, and attitudes that enabled the families she's related to by birth and by marriage, to remain together for a combined total of 224 years. Her family of origin started the Henderson Estate Company in 1890. This was the forerunner of the Sheraton Hotel Chain which her father co-founded. The Hendersons recently celebrated their 127th reunion. Perdue Farms, her family by marriage, began as a breakfast egg company in 1920, and will soon be celebrating its 100th anniversary.

The secret for the longevity of both families is: neither the Hendersons nor the Perdues left their family's legacy to chance. Using templates, checklists, activities, stories, and tips, Mitzi helps families design and maintain the culture that will help them stay together across the generations.